Lessons From the Field

A Common Sense Approach
for
Effective Hotel Sales

LESSONS FROM THE FIELD

A COMMON-SENSE APPROACH TO EFFECTIVE HOTEL SALES

Howard Feiertag
& John Hogan

JM Press • Brentwood, TN

Lessons From the Field

ISBN: 0-9713019-0-5
Library of Congress Control Number: 2001094153

John Hogan
johnjhogan@yahoo.com

Howard Feiertag
howardf@vt.edu

Published by JM Press, Brentwood, TN 37024

Dedications

Dedications are a personal moment of reflection. Thank you for letting me share these with you.

Professionally

To the Averys of Vermont - Borden, Louise and Allen.

Independent minded hoteliers who shared their passion and enthusiasms with many people over the years.

Personally

To Kathleen — who always encourages me to keep reaching.

—John Hogan

Preface

Nashville, Tennessee.
5:30 am ....a March morning, 1993

The loud sound broke the silence and we all know that sense of the unknown when the phone rings at such an early hour. This fortunately was not a medical or family emergency, but rather a seminar leader who was "snowed in" at a Virginia airport. He asked me to pinch-hit for him at a national sales presentation he was scheduled to make five hours later. I was scheduled to speak on housekeeping operations management at the same time for the same hotel company, but the group's leaders and I managed to find a way to have both programs delivered to their attendees. Delivering the very personalized sales message of my co-author was not an easy task, (and remember I had to try to read his 55 pages of faxed handwritten notes to keep on target with his handouts) but it worked.

That is what this book is all about – sharing what works!

Howard and I have known each other for more than twenty years now and I value the insight to hospitality sales he shares with the readers of his columns and those who attend his seminars. I am honored to co-author his first full-length book.

This book is a collaborative effort of two hoteliers with different backgrounds and experiences who have worked with a wide range of brands and types of hotels. It is our goal to provide you with some of the "common sense approaches" we have used and seen in our careers to date.

We hope you enjoy **Lessons from the Field** and we thank you for sharing your time with us.

--John Hogan

◆ ◆ ◆ ◆ ◆

Bricks and mortar, whether manu-factured 50 years ago or yesterday, make only a relatively small contri-bution to the success of the world's finest hotels. By and large, the single most important sales factor in the hospitality industry is the qual-ity of service provided.

Steve Marcus, President, Marcus Hotel Corporation

(quote found in Educational Institute's Hospitality for Sale)

◆ ◆ ◆ ◆ ◆

Howard Feiertag

Howard Feiertag (howardf@vt.edu), a well-known hospitality industry veteran with over 35 years in the industry, is on the Hospitality and Tourism Management faculty at Virginia Polytechnic Institute and State University.

Feiertag has an array of professional certifications and honors, including:

• A Charter member and recipient of the President's Award from Meeting Professionals International

• 1998 Educator of the Year by the Professional Convention Management Association

• 1999 inductee into the Convention Industry Council's Hall of Leaders

• 2001 appointment as a "Fellow" of the American Hotel & Lodging Association's Educational Institute and

• The 2001 recipient of the Arthur Landstreet Award from the Educational Institute (EI) of the AH & LA for significantly advancing the quality of hospitality education and training through his mentorship initiatives and lifetime commitment to training and development of hospitality professionals.

• Certified Meeting Professional (CMP)

• Certified Hospitality Marketing Executive (CHME)

• Certified Hotel Administrator (CHA)

• A "Fellow" and lifetime member of the Institute of Certified Travel Agents (ICTA)

• An honoree of the Hospitality Sales and Marketing Association International's Hall of Fame.

He is the group and meetings editor for *Travel Trade* Publications, a monthly columnist for *Corporate & Incentive Travel* magazine, and has been a regular columnist for *Hotel & Motel Management* magazine since 1980. A faculty member of the MPI Institute for over 15 years, he has conducted educational and training programs for The Educational Institute, Hospitality Services of America, Virginia Tech Continuing Education Division and is a frequent presenter for hotel companies, meeting planner, and travel agent groups.

Howard Feiertag

John Hogan

John Hogan (johnjhogan@yahoo.com) is the Director of Education & Training for Best Western International, the world's largest hotel chain. A graduate of the University of Massachusetts, his background includes teaching college level courses as an adjunct professor for 20 years, while working with Sheraton, Hilton, Dunfey/Omni and independents hotels at all levels of management. ITT Sheraton recognized him for his work in operations, marketing and renovations with Worldwide Awards of Excellence for both personal and team efforts. A former volunteer President for both city and state hotel associations, he has been involved in hospitality education for many industry meetings, academic institutions and ownership groups. He is a Certified Hotel Administrator and a Master Hotel Supplier.

Prior to joining Best Western International in spring of 2000, he was the principal in an independent training & consulting group for more than 13 years. As Education and Training Director for Best Western International, his assignments include creating, planning and facilitating training workshops for Best Western owners, operators and headquarters staff through direct, personalized interaction and professional services. The E&T team also constantly researches cost-effective ways to collaborate with professional and educational partners

He has published more than 100 articles & columns on the hospitality industry and is a recipient of the Pearson Award for Excellence in Lodging Journalism by the American Hotel & Lodging Association. He is based in Phoenix, Arizona and is currently working on his advanced degrees.

John Hogan

Contents

Common Sense Thoughts on the Fundamentals

Common Sense Thoughts on The Tools Available to You

Common Sense Thoughts on Strategies to Make You Successful in Hotel Sales

Common Sense Thoughts on Making your Sales Efforts Work

Common Sense Thoughts on Communication

Common Sense Thoughts on Perspective

Common Sense Thoughts on the Inner Workings of a Successful Hotel Sales Effort

Closing Thoughts

Appendix

Introduction

When we first discussed the format of this book, we tried to visualize the probable audience. Would it be sales staff at medium size hotels? General managers? Owner/operators of smaller properties? College audiences? Academics? Hourly staff?

We decided to write as we have conducted ourselves in most of our business, professional lives. Both of us have written columns and articles for industry publications and we wanted to include some of the approaches and messages that have been well received. We also wanted to use real life examples we had either personally experienced in the field or from stories shared in seminars and workshops.

We wanted to be open, to-the-point and to use understandable, conversational language. By that, we meant we would try to stay away from industry buzzwords and acronyms, but would keep the messages targeted and hopefully interesting. While we have included an appendix on those industry buzzwords for additional clarification, we recognized that many staff and guests may not understand the differences between a "connecting" and an "adjoining" room or who gets paid a service charge. We hope this book will remove some of the unnecessary "mystique".

The world of hospitality sales has changed from what it was when we first started in the industry, but it has retained much of what it always was. The needs for personal contact, for a sincere handshake, a warm smile and a personal commitment have never been greater.

Our goal was to share ideas and concepts that we know work. We believe our format of conversational writing to be comfortable, understandable and effective.

Thank you for taking the time to share our experiences through Lessons from the Field and we wish you much success in hotel sales.

John Hogan　　　　　　　　Howard Feiertag

Common Sense Thoughts
on
the Fundamentals

◆ ◆ ◆ ◆ ◆

I think the original basic axioms of sales promotion still hold true. Make a plan, demonstrate and follow the plan, and then monitor the plan at every step.

A. Peter DiTullio, retired President, Hyatt International Corporation

(quote found in Educational Institute's Hospitality for Sale)

◆ ◆ ◆ ◆ ◆

Chapter 1

Identifying Your Customers

The commitment of dedicated service providers means delivering a product or service. The intent of this conversational-style book is to offer insight and options into the sales efforts of those products and services.

We find it astonishing when we ask hoteliers who their customers are and they say "everyone." While hotels do service "everyone", the fact is that there are very few (if any) hotels that can honestly cater to all markets.

The basics may be defined like this: the hospitality industry offers and rents overnight accommodations and services. Since "everyone" needs overnight lodging at some point, everyone is a potential customer, right? No, wrong! Maintaining profit margins (while improving in the late 1990s) has been compared to requiring the agility and flexibility of a gymnast walking a balance beam.

National (and now truly global) companies have done their best to insure market saturation to be "all things to all people." A few franchise companies today dominate control of the brands known to most travelers and it is becoming more difficult to track ownership of brands and notable distinctions between brands.

Full service, mid-price range hotels (like many Best Westerns, Holiday Inns, Marriott Courtyards, Four Points, Ramada Inns/Plazas, etc.) come perhaps closest to offering what most people need and want. Even within those brands there are tremendous ranges of rates, specifics of services, staff capabilities and more.

Who are your customers? They must be identified literally daily, as most use our services for a short period of time (usually less than four days, unless you are in a resort or extended-stay property). They must have easy access to learning about your services, be able to confirm their request (frequently sight unseen by both parties) through a growing range of mediums (Central Reservation Offices, the Internet, travel partners like airlines, car rentals, travel agents, tour brokers, corporate and in-house travel managers, affinity services and programs that resell at deep discounts).

And there is one more means of access - directly with your hotel. That is what this book is about – the direct contact.

Knowing who your customers are requires recognizing what they want and need quickly or often even before they do. Southwest Airlines made air travel affordable for many who had never traveled by air regularly by looking at customer frustrations (delays, poor airline food, expensive tickets, confusing routes) and by overcoming them. Hampton Inns was able to launch its brand in the most challenging of times in our industry (the late 1980s-early 1990s) by convincing its franchisees that the 100% Guarantee program would be as effective as it has been. Both of these companies (and others) listened to what other people's customers were saying and did something about it. Many more airlines and hotel companies have continued to do what they have always done and watched as their market share and customers were literally "stolen" by solid product and effective salesmanship.

Herb Kelleher of Southwest Airlines has been described in almost every business publication as a maverick, an independent spirit and a sales person with incredible drive and initiative. Now retired Hampton Inns CEO Ray Shultz learned the lesson from the 1980's less-than-successful Holiday Inns "No

Surprises" program. (Shultz was with Holiday Inns at the time of that program.) "No Surprises" was not successful because the Holiday Inn franchisees were "told" they would participate in the program. Many of them did not embrace the idea and it was short-lived.

Ray, on the other hand, "sold" the concept of Hampton Inn's 100% Guarantee as a personal commitment to be made by existing and prospective franchisees for it to work. Other companies had tried variations of this before, but no one had tried to make it part of the "culture" of a major company in the hospitality field. Today, a number of service providers have found this commitment to be an essential part of their sales message.

◆ ◆ ◆ ◆ ◆

THE WORLD'S SHORTEST SALES COURSE

#1 Know their business

#2 Know your stuff.

(Bits & Pieces Vol.T/No.23)

◆ ◆ ◆ ◆ ◆

Chapter 2

Recognizing the Many Ways to Reach and Influence Potential Customers

Skip Boyer, the Director of Executive Communications at Best Western International and the senior member of his team, introduces a simple but wonderful story when his department is explaining the differences between the various forms of marketing at the company's regular orientations for owners and management new to Best Western.

He opens his presentation by asking the group if they understand the differences between "publicity" and "public relations." Answers vary by group, but the following story illustrates the various components.

He begins by saying, "Let's imagine you are about to announce to the world the grand opening of your brand new hotel, the Best Western Anywhere Inn. You run a full-page ad in the local paper inviting everyone. This is "advertising," he says.

"Now it just so happens the circus is in town, and you decide to hire the elephant to carry a giant billboard announcing your opening. This is promotion", Skip will say. The problem is that something frightens the elephant and he tramples the garden at the nearby competitive hotel and the picture of the elephant, your billboard and the damage makes the front page of the business section. This is publicity (and not the right kind).

If, and Skip will pause here for a moment, the hotel general manager goes to the competitive hotel's manager with a sincere apology (accompanied by a check to cover the damage, it is assumed) and convinces that manager to attend the grand opening party, that is salesmanship. When the business section features its' next photo of your hotel, it is with you, the competitive GM and the elephant, with all apparently forgiven. That photo and the accompanying story are public relations.

A major objective of hotel owners, managers and sales professionals is to profitably provide hospitality services to as many guests as possible. Recognizing the differences in the various components of the sales and marketing efforts will undoubtedly make that service provider more focused on net results, guest satisfaction and profitability, rather than on headlines.

Chapter 3

The Difference Between Marketing and Sales

M any people use the terminology "marketing" and "sales" as having the same meaning. Is there a difference between Marketing and Sales? The answer is a resounding "YES!" Both are critical to matching your hotel's features and services to the guest who wants and needs them, but the two words do not have the same meaning.

Marketing includes identifying and determining customers' wants and needs, and then providing them at a profit. One of your property's marketing functions may be your sales staff and sales efforts, but there are many other marketing activities as well.

Marketing incorporates:

• Research – Determining who and understanding the needs of the characteristics of guests who come into your marketplace (business, leisure, meeting, contract, etc.) How will the marketplace trends affect your profitability in serving those guests? How do you keep track of your competition? What are their marketing efforts and how do you exceed them?

• Promotions – Planning programs and special events that your hotel sponsors or participates in that bring attention to the guests you identified in research as probably being drawn to your type of hotel and its' service levels. The goal for promotions is to increase traffic and revenues, or sometimes to trial run a new service

• Advertising – Communicating and delivering your paid message in ways you believe will be effective, including radio, print, cable, TV, internet, etc.

• Public relations – Being involved in activities aimed at spreading the word and improving relations in your local community in a fashion that highlights the goodwill features of your hotel

• Pricing – Actively and regularly keeping your offerings at a competitive and profitable level, including using yield management strategies, special programs and partnering with other companies that may or may not be in the hospitality sector

• Publicity – highlighting the best side of your hotel, sometimes even in stressful situations such as an emergency, a fire or negative event that may occur at your hotel

Sales is part of the marketing efforts, but specifically includes:

• Personal efforts to sell the property's services

• Direct telephone solicitation in qualifying prospects

• Tele-marketing efforts to match prospects' needs with the hotels features, resulting in confirmed business.

Creating and implementing the marketing plan – this is one of the most critical portions of marketing, as this planning cycle often means success or failure.

During the marketing planning process, the decision on how to position the property in the marketplace is key to the sales effort. By this, we mean how prospects might view your hotel. Do they see you as the first choice meeting site or as property that houses guests who are having their meetings at the convention center? Are you a complete service resort or an inexpensive option on the way to the destination? Are you a first or last choice airport option for airline crews or distressed passengers?

These questions are asked by potential guests, whether the property's management and sales team considers them or not. The truly successful hotels and companies evaluate their services as compared to the marketplace and then use all the marketing tools they can to communicate that positioning to the marketplace.

Included in the positioning analysis for both the Marketing and Sales efforts usually include:

• Understanding the "big" picture, which means detailed research of clients likely to use your hotel. If your hotel belongs to a membership, referral or franchise organization, substantial overview research probably has already been completed and is available to you for the asking.

• Long-term goals may reflect planned expansions, renovations or upgrading of services. Reaching your positioning target profitably is critical.

• Short-term goals are usually the current year or less and reflect your hotel's performance as compared to the local marketplace. It is essential to participate in the national reporting services, such as Smith Travel Research, because that is the only effective way to accurately see how you are actually competing with your competitors.

• Ongoing evaluation of proper positioning the property usually follows analysis of the short-term performance as compared to the rest of your marketplace. If you are way ahead of everyone else in your direct market competitive set, you may have the option to upgrade your customer target and reach higher revenues. If you are substantially under performing, then it is clearly time to evaluate your direct sales efforts to correct the shortfall.

• Quotas are frequently tied to monthly revenue goals and the most profitable mix of business should yield bonuses or commissions to sales staff who can demonstrate they can bring in new business, while retaining existing clients.

At many smaller properties (under 100 rooms), the owner or general manager may pursue the marketing end of things. Depending on the circumstances, they should initiate sales as well.

For the medium sized property (100-250 rooms), most will have a sales department. This could consist of a Director of Sales (DOS), Catering Manager, and one or more Sales Managers. The DOS may be involved with marketing, meaning that this position will assist owners, managers and/or a management company in devising a marketing plan and agenda.

Sales managers should have limited involvement in marketing, instead, concentrating their efforts to personal and direct sales. This means that their time will be spent conducting outside sales calls and attending community events. Sales managers will frequently conduct tele-marketing or tele-sales to set up "warm calls" prior to conducting outside sales calls.

Often there is not an adequate separation of Sales and Marketing at both smaller and medium sized properties. A sales manager cannot effectively sell the property if their time is being utilized to develop marketing plans and research.

The large property (250 rooms or more) may have a similar set to the medium sized property. Here, there will frequently be a larger number of sales managers and there may even be a Director of Marketing. It is even more critical then that the Sales Managers do not get bogged down in marketing activities, but instead concentrate their effort at what they were hired to do ....SALES! If your property has a Sales Manager that spends the majority of the time in the office, then that activity needs to be re-evaluated and re-assigned because a critical part of the marketing or sales machinery is not being used properly.

There are times that the sales person's input is needed when creating Sales and Marketing Plans, packages, etc. Brainstorming between the two segments of the department is an important aspect at that time. Once the ideas have been gathered, it is the marketing department/owner/managers job then to set the goals and objectives. It is the sales departments job to assist with finding ways to accomplish those goals and objectives, and to make it all happen.

◆ ◆ ◆ ◆ ◆

Zig Ziglar tells of visiting the Washington monument. As he and his party approached the monument, he heard a guide announcing loudly that there would be a two-hour wait to ride the elevator to the top of the monument. However, with a smile on his face the guide then said, "There is no one waiting to go to the top if you are willing to take the stairs."

(King Duncan, *King's Treasury of Dynamic Humor*, Seven Worlds Press)

Chapter 4

The Value of Outside Resources

In today's quickly changing marketplace, the person responsible for sales frequently needs additional assistance. Smaller properties (those under 100 rooms that may not have a specific person dedicated solely to sales) often have an even greater challenge.

Many associations and organizations, at the local, regional or national levels, exist as resources today that can offer tremendous assistance at no or comparatively little cost. Membership in these organizations can vary. In some, hoteliers are the primary category of members. Some others include hotel sales professionals as allied or associate members. For those hotels that are part of a membership, referral or franchise organization, there are usually internal resources available. Independent hotels have to decide on their own which organizations will have the most positive impact on that independent hotel.

The size and complexity of a property may dictate the level of sophistication required to assist efforts to effectively reach more potential customers.

Some notable resources (listed in alphabetical order) include:

American Bus Association – <u>www.buses.org</u>

1100 New York Ave. N.W. Suite 100,   Washington,   D.C. 20005-3934

Phone: 202-842-1645   Fax: 202-842-0850

E-mail: abainfo@buses.org

The American Bus Association, which is the trade association of the intercity bus industry, represents the motor coach industry's interests in Washington, D.C. It also facilitates relationships between North American motor coach and tour companies, all related segments of the travel and supplier industries. ABA promotes travel by motor coach to consumers and represents approximately 800 motor coach and tour companies in the United States and Canada. Its members operate charter, tour, regular route, airport express, special operations and contract services (commuter, school, transit) and use hotels of all brands, sizes and locations. Another 2,300 member organizations represent the travel and tourism industry and suppliers of bus products and services who work in partnership with the North American motor coach industry. ABA has a total membership of more than 3,000 strong, making a major force for many hospitality companies.

American Hotel & Lodging Association   www.ahla.org

1201 New York Avenue, NW, #600, Washington, DC 20005-3931

Tel: 202-289-3100 Fax: 202-289-3199

E-mail: information center@ahlaonline.org

The American Hotel & Lodging Association (AH&LA) is the largest national trade association for the U.S. hotel and lodging industry. AH&LA provides its member lodging properties with resources to operate more efficiently and more profitably. As the national organization, AH&LA is comprised of 52 member state associations, including Washington, D.C., and New York City. Lodging properties — from small economy motels to large convention hotels, to luxurious resorts to vacation ownership properties — first join their state association and then automatically become enrolled in AH&LA.

Moving in the 1990s from New York to Washington, DC to be able to better present the industry's views to law makers, this is the US national lodging coalition. Membership cost will vary, depending on size of the property, but most state and local associations are linked to the national. The Educational Institute (www.ei-ahla.org) is an excellent resource for information, products and services as the AH&LA training arm. AH&LA members receive a substantial discount from the catalogue prices.

At the national level, AH&LA lobbies federal legislators who make key decisions about your business and its bottom line (e.g., labor shortage issues and OSHA regulations). At the state level, the benefits offered may include free legal and accounting services, state law updates, discount vendor programs, employee benefit and workers' compensation discounts, credit cards processing discounts, and more.

State (Provincial) Hotel & Lodging Associations – Most, if not all, are located in the state or provincial capital in order to be able to lobby legislators. There are also local or regional associations in most areas. The smaller the organization, the more local the issues that will be addressed and the resources are available on a case-by-case study, but many are excellent.

American Society of Association Executives -
www.asaenet.org/main/
1575 I St. N.W., Washington, D.C. 20005
Phone: 202-626-2723 Fax: 202-371-8825

ASAE, known as the association of associations, is considered the advocate for the nonprofit sector. The society is dedicated to advancing the value of voluntary associations to society and supporting the professionalism of the individuals who lead them. Founded in 1920 as the American Trade Association Executives, with 67 charter members, ASAE now has more than 25,000 individual members who manage leading trade, professional, and philanthropic associations. ASAE represents approximately 10,000 associations serving more than 287 million people and companies worldwide and vendors that offer products and services to the association community.

Most states and provinces have chapters of ASAE and these regional associations use hotels of all sizes and brands for conventions, regional meetings, board and committee retreats and banquets.

American Society of Training & Development – www.astd.org
1640 King Street, Box 1443 Alexandria, Virginia, 22313-2043, USA
Phone: 703.683.8100 - 800.628.2783 - Fax: 703.683.1523
E-mail: Customercare@astd.org

Founded in 1944, ASTD is the world's premier professional association and leading resource on workplace learning and performance issues. ASTD provides information, research, analysis and practical information derived from its own research, the knowledge and experience of its members, its conferences, expositions, seminars, publications and the coalitions and partnerships it has built through research and policy work. ASTD's membership includes more than 70,000 people, working in the field of workplace performance in 100 countries worldwide. Its leadership and members work in more than 15,000 multinational corporations, small and medium sized businesses, government agencies, colleges and universities. ASTD members use hotels of all sizes and brands for training programs, workshops, seminars, regional meetings, retreats and banquets.

American Society of Travel Agents – www.astanet.com

1101 King St., Suite 200   Alexandria,   VA   22313-2043
Phone: 703-739-2782   Fax: 703-684-8319

ASTA, short for the American Society of Travel Agents, is the world's largest association of travel professionals. Over 26,000 member agencies include travel agents and the companies whose products they sell such as tours, cruises, hotels, car rentals, etc. Their web site states they are the leading advocates for travel agents, the travel industry and the traveling public. These professionals are most frequently paid by commission and use hotels of all sizes and brands for individual and group travel, including conventions, regional meetings, vacations and combinations of the above.

Asian American Hotel Owners Association – www.aahoa.com

66 Lenox Pointe NE Atlanta, GA 30324
Phone: 404-816-5759   Fax: 404-816-6260
E-mail: aahoa@aol.com

The AAHOA web site states the association provides an active forum in which Asian American Hotel Owners, through an exchange of ideas with a unified voice, can communicate, interact, and secure their proper position within the hospitality industry, and be a source of inspiration by promoting professionalism and excellence through education and community involvement.

Chambers of Commerce and Convention and Visitors Bureaus

These are local organizations, whose goals are to bring visitors, tourists, organized meetings and conventions to your particular city or town. Larger cities have staffs dedicated to this goal, with promotional and advertising budgets. Smaller towns frequently rely on the Chamber of Commerce to blend this visitor solicitation with other assignments. Check with your local hotel association for details. (see also IACVB)

Hotel Sales & Marketing Association International – www.hsmai.org

400 K St. N.W. Suite 810   Washington, D.C. 20005
Phone: 202-789-0089   Fax: 202-789-1725

HSMAI is the largest international association of travel sales and marketing professionals, welcoming over 5,000 hospitality sales and marketing executives annually who look to the association as the single-most important resource in their continued professional development.

There are member chapters in most metropolitan areas, with many HSMAI programs offered throughout the US and Canada. HSMAI University and an annual training summit are always well received by members. The professional certifications of CHSP (Certified Hospitality Sales Professional) and CHME (Certified Hospitality Meeting Executive) are granted through HSMAI

Institute of Certified Travel Agents   www.icta.com

148 Linden Street, PO Box 812059,
Wellesley, MA 02482: 800.542.4282 fax: 781.237.3860.

The Institute of Certified Travel Agents (ICTA) is an international, nonprofit organization that educates and certifies travel industry professionals at all career stages. Since its inception in 1964, ICTA's mission has been to increase professionalism within the travel industry and to create national standards of excellence for travel professionals through its educational programs. ICTA's programs encompass all career stages for the travel professional from entry level to executive. These programs include certification, national entry-level credentials, destination-focused training, leading textbook programs and Licensed Schools. These professionals work for travel agencies that are most frequently paid by commission and use hotels of all sizes and brands for individual and group travel, including conventions, regional meetings, vacations and combinations of the above.

International Association of Convention & Visitors Bureaus – www.IACVB.org

2025 M St. N.W. Suite 500   Washington, D.C. 20036 Phone: 202-296-7888   Fax: 202-296-7889 E - m a i l : info@iacvb.org

The International Association of Convention & Visitor Bureaus represents over 1,100 professional members from over 480 bureaus in 30 countries. The association was founded in 1914 to promote sound professional practices in he solicitation and servicing of meetings and conventions. IACVB's member bureaus represent all significant travel/tourism-related businesses at the local and regional level. They also serve as the primary contact point for their destination for a broad universe of convention, meeting, and tour professionals. (see also local Chambers of Commerce, Convention and Visitors Bureaus)

Meeting Professionals International – www.mpiweb.org/home.asp

4455 LBJ Freeway, Suite 1200   Dallas, TX 75244-5903. Phone: 972-702-3000   Fax:972-702-3070

Meeting Professionals International (MPI) is the premier educational, technological and networking resource in the industry. With more than 17,000 members in 64 countries with 58 chapters and six clubs, MPI is committed to enhancing the overall quality of meetings by ensuring the professional development and growth of its membership. MPI members collectively account for a total of $10.9 billion expended on meetings per year, representing some 610,662 conclaves held throughout the world.

These individuals control an average annual budget of $1.4 million and are each responsible for booking at least 1,200 room nights per year at hotels of varying size and brand. The association offers superior educational programming, timely and topical communication, an extensive Resource Center and numerous forums for peer interaction. Earning the CMP (Certified Meeting Planner) is part of the MPI programs. Belonging to local chapters of MPI is critical in achieving recognition and business from this source.

National Association of Catering Executives – www.nace.net
5565 Sterret Place, Suite 328   Columbia, MD 21044
410-997-9055   Fax410-997-8834   esuddath@nace.net

NACE is the oldest and largest professional association that addresses all aspects of the catering industry. Through the collective efforts of members, local chapters, committees and Foundation, this organization tries to be at the forefront of issues that directly affecting catering. NACE offers practical tips to provide better service to clients, to recognition and marketing programs that enhance the credibility and professionalism of the field. NACE features educational programs, works on establishing standards, ethics and is involved in legislative monitoring.

NACE has over 40 chapters offering monthly meetings that feature nationally renowned speakers, educational programs, idea sharing and networking. Chapter involvement provides an opportunity to work on community service projects and voice your opinion about issues that affect you locally and nationally. The NACE Educational Conference held each summer is the largest event in the world dedicated exclusively to the professional caterer and industry suppliers. Nationally recognized speakers and catering professionals present a comprehensive educational program and social events showcase the best and brightest in menu planning, food preparation, service, presentation and decorations. NACE also offers Certification, a Membership Directory, Leadership Training, a Research Foundation and annual Awards Programs.

National Tour Association – www.ntaonline.com

Executive Office - 800-682-8886
546 East Main Street, Lexington, KY 40508
Fax 859-226-4414

The Mission Statement of The National Tour Association says it strives to provide unsurpassed business opportunities, knowledge and information to businesses involved in tour operator packaged travel. NTA strives to be the preferred association of packaged travel businesses. The annual NTA convention attracts more than 1,000 qualified brokers who book literally millions of dollars of business for the next 12-24 months at scheduled appointments with hotel representatives.

Ontario Motor Coach Association – www.omca.com

4141 Yonge St. Suite 306   Toronto, ON Canada M2P 2A8
Phone: 416-229-6622   Fax: 416-229-6281
E-mail: info@omca.com

The Ontario Motor Coach Association (OMCA) is a trade association representing the interests of Ontario's intercity bus industry. On behalf of our 1,200 members, including 80 motor coach and 80 travel and tour operations, the OMCA works with all government levels to highlight the achievements of the province's intercity bus business. OMCA members provide scheduled, charter, tour, contract, transit and school bus services throughout the province and US charter tours throughout the United States.

Professional Convention Management Association
www.pcma.org

2301 South Lake Shore Drive, Suite 1001, Chicago, IL 60616-1419
Phone 312.423.7262 Fax: 312.423.7222
meetingservices@pcma.org

As ASAE is the association for associations, PCMA serves the association community by enhancing the effectiveness of meetings, conventions, and exhibitions through member and industry education and to promote the value of the meetings industry to the general public. Their web site lists PCMA's Principles of Professional and Ethical Conduct as " represent(ing) the highest levels of professional and ethical behavior in the convention and meetings industry. The association has adopted these Principles of Professional and Ethical Conduct and its members use them as standards of honorable behavior by which they may evaluate their relationships with their organizations, suppliers, and colleagues."

PCMA meetings are widely regarded as the most comprehensive and up-to-date educational events in the industry. Each January, PCMA hosts thousands of meetings industry professionals at an innovative educational gathering. This annual event offers nearly 100 educational sessions for all levels of experience, pre-convention institutes for additional in-depth training, and a wide variety of opportunities for networking and community service.

There are chapters at many locations throughout the US and Canada and the association uses many hotel sites for a variety of different meetings and functions.

Society of Corporate Meeting Planners – www.scmp.org

2965 Flowers Rd. South, Suite 105 Atlanta, GA 30341
Phone: 770-457-9212 Fax: 770-458-3314

SCMP is a community of corporate meeting professionals committed to serving its members and employers through quality education and an open forum exchanging information & ideas. SCMP is a volunteer-driven organization. 2001 marks over thirty years in existence, making SCMP a well-established member of the Hospitality and Meetings Industry.

Society of Government Meeting Planners www.sgmp.org

908 King St., Lower Level Alexandria, VA ·
Phone: 703.549.0892 Fax 703.549.0708

SGMP is a professional organization of persons involved in planning government meetings, either on a full or part-time basis, and those individuals who supply services to government planners. The stated objectives are to improve the quality and promote the cost effectiveness of government meetings by improving the knowledge and expertise of individuals in the planning and management of government meetings through education, training, and industry relationships.

The Society of Government Meeting Professionals was established in October 1981 in Washington, DC. Organizers of government meetings saw a need for a forum in which to discuss mutual objectives and techniques for conducting business meetings of the government. They sought to create an opportunity to meet on common ground with the providers of meeting services and facilities to review the latest trends in planning and implementing these events. Today, the Society spans the nation with 26 chapters and more than 2,700 members.

Represented in SGMP's membership are employees of federal, state, county and city government, as well as associations of governmental employees and government agencies. The

Society of Government Meeting Professionals is the only national organization in the United States dedicated exclusively to improving the knowledge and expertise of individuals in the planning and execution of government meetings through education, training, and industry relationships. A national board of directors and officers elected by the membership manages SGMP. Affiliate chapters elect local leadership and conduct monthly meetings in their respective areas

Society of Government Travel Professionals

www.government-travel.org
6935 Wisconsin Avenue, Bethesda, MD 20815
301-654-8595   Fax 301-654-6663

SGTP (formerly Society Of Travel Agents In Government/STAG) is the national, non-profit education forum for all components of the $20 billion Government travel market. Since 1984, SGTP has been an all encompassing and inclusive association for Government travel/finance managers, suppliers and travel agents-whose primary objective is to facilitate and promote best practices and a spirit of innovation in Government travel. This group is directly or indirectly responsible for directing many government clients to hotels of all sizes and types, as the very diversified Government travel market has many facets and approaches. SGTP is dedicated to helping you answer the many questions about this multi-faceted market by increase knowledge of and professionalism in Government travel management.

The semi-annual Education Conferences help you develop and implement your Government travel program; identify standards and trends in the industry to sharpen your marketing strategies; and, put you in contact with key Government and contractor personnel and travel industry leaders. There are also Individualized Workshops geared to your specific needs and interests. Workshops on civilian and DoD Government policies, geographic interest groups, developing your leisure program, hotel/supplier workshops, and developing your Government travel operations/sales program-among others. SGTP has an On-Line service (www.Government-travel.org), Publications and continual networking opportunities.

Travel Industry Association of America –
www.tia.org/home.asp

1100 New York Ave. Suite 450   Washington, D.C. 20005-3934
Phone: 202-408-8422   Fax: 202-408-1255
E-mail: feedback@tia.org

The Travel Industry Association of America (TIA), in existence since 1941, is a Washington DC based, non-profit association that represents and speaks for the common interests and concerns of all components of the U.S. travel industry. It is viewed as a recognized leader in promoting and facilitating increased travel to and within the United States in order to make America the world's number one tourism destination. It is an authoritative and recognized source of research, analysis and forecasting for the entire industry and frequently acts as the primary spokesperson to the domestic and international media.

◆ ◆ ◆ ◆ ◆

Outlook on Planning & Effort

"The will to win is important, but the will to prepare is vital"

Penn State Football Coach Joe Paterno

Penn State has one of the best athletic records in the nation, with a very high rate of first team, academic All-American graduates each year

◆ ◆ ◆ ◆ ◆

Common Sense Thoughts
on
the Tools Available to You

◆ ◆ ◆ ◆ ◆

Quick reactions to the changes in the business cycle and preferences of our guests are essential to maintaining high occupancies. Innovations, particularly those which improve occupancies over traditionally slack periods such as weekends, have also contributed to our continuing high occupancy rates.

—*James Durbin, former President, Marriott Hotels*

(quote found in Educational Institute's Hospitality for Sale)

◆ ◆ ◆ ◆ ◆

Chapter 5

The Ten Most Important Characteristics of Successful Sales Professionals in the Hospitality Field

1. **They are motivated to succeed.** Their personal drive is to meet and exceed goals or quotas regularly.

2. **They recognize the value of that all-important first impression.**

3. **They genuinely like people and try to be liked themselves.**

4. **They sincerely want to meet the needs of both their customers and their own employer.** This is not always easy to do, as prices; availability of space or facilities, seasonality and the ever-changing mind-sets in a truly global marketplace offers mixed demands.

5. **They are competitive.** They recognize they may be part of a sales or management team, but they intend to be the best on the team.

6. **They don't take "no" personally.**

7. **They most likely had a mentor or role model they still try to emulate or whose strategies they follow.** They are likely to become mentors themselves, if given the opportunity.

8. They know their product and that of their competitors inside and out. They constantly evaluate their own offerings and match them correctly to their customers.

9. They constantly try to improve their own skill sets. They attend formal seminars or classes, use the Internet and read books. They listen to skill related audiocassettes/CDs while in their cars on the way to their next appointment.

10. They are service oriented. They take pride in ownership of their account and make certain the service is delivered as promised. While there may be someone at the hotel assigned to serve the banquet, to check the group in or to drive the van to the University or Corporate Center, the most successful sales professionals are likely to be double-checking the details. This is not to micro-manage or second-guess the other staff members, but they feel that sense of pride and their customers show their appreciation with repeat bookings.

Chapter 6

Knowing Where Your Business Originates

This message is painstakingly simple, yet is ignored by all of us at least some of the time. We are often so busy looking for the "new" customer/guest that we forget the existing ones.

Where is the point of origin or where do your current guests come from? Who are the key reservation makers or referral points? If you don't know the answers, then you are missing an opportunity to improve your service, sales, your guest satisfaction scores and your profitability. All four (service, sales, satisfaction, profitability) tie together. Most staff like to care for regular guests, most regular guests feel appreciated and rate your business more highly, and profits rise with satisfied guests.

Each manager (sales and general manager) should know the top ten local accounts. Those managers should also work with the reservations team (or front desk in smaller hotels) and learn the long distance reservation makers. Most reservation systems of referral groups and franchise companies have access to a "source of business" report that can trend shifts in referral sources. A report is only worthwhile if someone takes the responsibility and pride to "own" it by a regular review session.

Using account contacts from these local and business source referral reports, managers should call on and/or visit a pre-set number of accounts weekly. The calls need not be long, but they need to regularly say "thanks for the business" and "we have a new (event or service)" coming up this month we knew your visitors would like" and "is there anything else we do to serve your lodging (or banquet or meeting) needs?" If you don't keep saying thank you and asking for the business regularly, your competition will.

Local and referral contacts can be used to create frequent traveler or secretary's clubs, to find potential leads for banquets, social functions, holiday gift lists and more. Creative managers know how to say "thanks", while also asking, "how about sending some more business our way?"

Chapter 7

Finding Business Leads
Can Be Easier Than You Think

Success in sales is often a result of developing good business leads' and some salespeople believe they must travel far and wide to track them down. The truth is, there are business leads right on your hotel's premises and perhaps more than you'd find by going out of town.

Here are four excellent ways to develop business leads without even leaving your office:

Current Guests

People who stay at your property are prime prospects for other types of business, such as meetings, conferences or social activities. A quick check of the reservation cards or your property management's guest history feature will reveal which guests are regular repeats or that may be logical prospects for more business.

Many hotels use a simple front desk promotional activity to gather business cards in a briefcase or glass bowl. The incentive for the guest is to win the monthly drawing for whatever you choose to give away. The incentive for the hotel is create a database of guests or locals meeting guests in your hotel. Look for corporate officers, association representatives, sales managers, personnel managers, etc. They may be in a position to decide where to hold their next meeting or where to send their overnight guests.

Employees of Your Hotel

Everybody belongs to some kind of organization, such as a church, garden club, bowling team, PTA, educational group - the list goes on and on.

Salespeople should take advantage of this by meeting with housekeepers, desk agents, accounting staff, bell staff/van drivers, restaurant and bar employees — anyone who works at the property. Ask them for their help in providing leads for meetings and social events.

Incentive programs provide the answer to the "what's in it for me" question asked by some employees. The 1990s provided tremendous employment opportunities for many hourly staff and they sometimes require reminders of the need for teamwork. Offer employees dinner for two at the restaurant of their choice, a weekend at the hotel, or a cash award based on the revenue generated as a result of the lead. There's a hidden benefit to having employees provide leads, which is improved staff moral.

Almost immediately, you'll see employees become more involved in working together. Just having salespeople speaking to other staff members will do the trick. The message here is, "Everybody sells."

Existing Files

The most likely and best source of leads is already at everyone's fingertips — right in the file drawer or the computer's memory. Unfortunately, files get buried so deep after guests depart or after a conference or meeting that no one takes the trouble to book the group again - until it is too late and the competition has made personal contact and "sold" them. Going through a few files each day is a good way to generate business from groups or regular guests that have booked your property in the past. If they had a positive experience at your hotel once, there's a strong possibility that they'd be glad to return. All you have to do is ask them!

Newspapers (hometown or regional)

Many of us read a newspaper at some point during the day. But does anyone read them with the purpose of developing business leads? There's a difference between simply reading a newspaper and reading it with a specific purpose in mind.

Try an experiment. Ask three or four people to review a local newspaper for anything that might lead to room business, meetings, parties, and dining room and bar business, etc. See who can find the most leads. You'll be astounded by the results. The "readers' will come up with more sales leads than you can contact in a day. The idea, of course, is to train people to read the newspaper with the thought of looking for business. Once they do this exercise, they'll look for leads every time they read a newspaper, and new business will be popping up automatically.

Who does the reading for the leads?

Everyone can do it. It can be assigned to different people on different days. Leads can be cut out and passed on to various department heads for follow-up. The sales manager should get the leads for group- meeting business; the front-office manager should get the leads for local contacts on room business; the catering manager gets the leads for social functions; the food and beverage manager gets the leads for restaurant and lounge business.

And the general manager's job is to make sure
the system works.

◆　◆　◆　◆　◆

The 4 Steps to Achievement

Planning

Preparation

Practice

Persistence

◆　◆　◆　◆　◆

Chapter 8

Keeping the Business You Have

In every size hotel operation, there are great potential and real opportunities for effective sales activity. The product and service level must be more than "minimum standard", but with the basics in place, there is a substantial amount of business that can be identified and captured at little to reasonable cost.

First of all, we have all read or heard that it is much easier to "keep" an existing customer/guest than to find a new one. Therefore, it is logical to recognize the value of keeping the business you already have. Repeat business is the foundation of both short and long term success in the hospitality/service industry. Today's guest (whether a first time guest who could become a repeat customer or an existing regular) must feel a sincere sense of welcome.

Take the time to regularly meet with your staff (the front desk team, the person who sets up continental breakfast, and all of your guest contact team) to review and evaluate the services and amenities you now offer. These could include free coffee in the morning, personal attentiveness, a welcome packet of local information, a personal "thank you and welcome" note from the general manager, and much more.

Then discuss what your team might be able to add to make your hotel clearly different and more inviting than the competition. We all know how one chain used to include warm cookies and cold milk with turndown service.

Turndown service is not universal with all hotels (whether they are 2, 3 or 4 stars or diamonds), but offering fresh fruit, candy, easily produced home-made type cookies (from companies like Otis Spunkmeyer), fragrant, tasty popcorn and other ideas unique to your neighborhood can make your hotel much more appealing.

Guests do not necessarily know the best restaurants, movie theaters, or malls in the area. Easily accessible and available information on these and all of your community's offerings can bring a smile to a business or leisure traveler who is looking for that home town flavor. Your staff personalizing your hotel's personality and commitment to their guests reinforces the idea of encouraging guests to return to your hotel because they were made to feel welcome and special.

Chapter 9

Some Careful Digging Will Help Uncover Lots Of Profit

A salesperson's responsibility to management doesn't end with going out on sales calls. It's the generating of sales or, more aptly, of profitable sales that counts.

Being a professional in hotel sales comes from a continued process of making yourself aware of what's happening in the marketplace. Learn what the competition is doing. Learn what different group accounts need or want. Learn how to present your hotel's features. Learn about creative food and beverage functions and how to use them as selling tools.

Specifically, managers and salespeople should learn all they can about their property's business mix; they need to explore market segments that have more profit potential; they need to tap the potential of existing accounts; and they need to solicit accounts similar to the ones they're already servicing. Let's take a look at each area:

Business Mix

Salespeople need to meet with the general manager to examine the current mix of business. By analyzing how much business is being generated from each market segment, and at what rate, it will become obvious if a change in the mix is desired. Most properties have a system for recording this information daily. Aiming for 100% occupancy as the only goal no longer works – in today's market, we have to consider revenue per available room (RevPAR), the overall arrival/departure patterns and the level of service we are able to provide as well.

Typically, the market segments for most hotels (regardless of size) will include individual travelers, which will further break-down into those paying regular rate, certain negotiated rate corporate travelers and a variety of individuals participating in some kind of special discount program, such as seniors, AAA, government, etc.

Another market that will vary by hotel size, location and facilities will be the extent of group business. These may include associations, corporations, government, educational and/or group-tours.

The objective is to develop more business from the segments that bring in the best rate or could be more profitable in the operation. If the AAA individual rate is better than the group-tour rate and they have equal demand, then it is obvious that more effort should be put into selling individual AAA customers. If the group meetings market has more potential in revenue and rooms volume (whether the meeting is at your hotel, the convention center or at another site), then that is where the focus should be.

High Profit Market Segments

Some types of business generate more profit for a property than other types. Student tour groups, for example, may generate good room sales, but little in the way of food & beverage revenues. Youth sports' tournaments bring teams, parents and families that do provide F&B sales.

The objective here is to generate sales in market segments that not only rent rooms, but provide revenue to all property outlets and/or that we can influence to use our facilities at a time mutually beneficial to both the customer and the hotel.

Tapping Existing Accounts

There are many salespeople who make sales calls on their corporate accounts only to look for the individual business traveler. The potential for additional business from an existing account is great, but it requires the salesperson to learn as much as possible about the account and to ask questions like:

• Does the company have meetings? Who handles the meetings?

• Which other departments in the company have people visiting who may need over- night accommodations?

• Who takes care of the company/s social activities and holiday parties?

• To which clubs or trade groups do the company's executives belong? Can they influence a decision to bring a meeting to the property?

• Does the company use hotels in other cities? This question can allow you as the sales person in city A to help your client in city B. While you may not receive any direct and immediate revenue, you might be able to help your client and another hotel of your brand and/or management group. Networking requires the efforts of everyone, not just when you get something today.

Generally, an existing account can and will provide more business to a property if the right contact is made and business is solicited.

Similar Accounts

There is a tendency for similar businesses or accounts to do similar things. If, for example, a property does business with Army recruiting people for meetings and meals, it is likely that the Navy, Air Force and Marines are doing pretty much the same thing, somewhere else. If a property hosts a weekend conference of piccolo players, then it is probable that there are associations of drummers, piano players or violinists who have similar meetings. If there is a party for a new-car showing put on by one auto dealership, then there may be a similar party that could be solicited from other dealerships in the area.

Salespeople need to regularly look for ways of developing new business for rooms and food & beverage. Opportunities abound for all types of business. Knowing what's going on in the marketplace, checking on the competition and exploring new profit sources are important keys to success in sales.

And remember: be enthusiastic about what you're selling!

Chapter 10

Building New Business

Building new business requires common sense, but not always big advertising bucks. A number of things that hotels of any size or brand can do to find and build new business include:

- **Time Commitments** - Spending at least two hours per day by a sales person or a general manager who realizes that time spent in logical (pro-active) "selling" is substantially valuable to the business. This is long-term much more valuable than a short-term savings on payroll by having the sales or general manager do other tasks, such as covering the desk three days a week, serving all banquets or repairing leaking showers.

- **Cooperation with competition** - every hotel or inn will have its 100% occupancy days and our goal should be to achieve the #1 overflow hotel status. This is not just today - it also includes those advance dates when "sold-out" is anticipated. Getting to know, work with and help out competition is a logical and ethical business practice. This means the GM, the sales team, each shift on the front desk (including the night audit shift) should know their counterparts and help them every chance they get. Little " gifts" or "thank you's" such as a box of candy, flowers, pizza sent to the front desk, etc. (appropriate to the source) can make a huge difference.

- **Sales Calls** - 5 pro-active calls a day to area referral sources will make an unbelievable difference. A person

63

whose primary job is sales can make these calls, but a part time sales person or the GM of a smaller property can also make it. Think about it – 2 calls per day equal 10 per week, roughly 40 calls per month, or almost 500 per year. 5 calls per day equal 25 per week, roughly 100 calls per month, more than 1,000 per year.

Five hundred to 1,000 personal visits to people who are known to need lodging, food, or meeting services in your community will provide a very positive return on the investment of time.

Chapter 11

Recognizing the Value
of the "Small Meetings" Markets

Regardless of the size of a hotel today, it can substantially boost its' overnight rooms business and it's overall profitability by focusing on the small-meeting market.

Surveys taken at almost any time in recent history reflect that the most common type of business (or social) meetings involve less than 50 people. In times of budget cutting, local business meetings off-site frequently take the place of more exotic locations favored in times of plenty.

While many associations have their annual meetings in large convention hotels, most committee and board meetings can be housed in smaller properties that may not be in large cities. While these smaller meetings do not fill entire hotels, a block of 10-25 rooms for several nights can be a pleasant bonus, filling valleys in higher demand periods.

Most hotels have at least some space that can be used for meetings. It could be multi-use space, such as that used for breakfast or social hours. It can be a lounge that is used only in the evening. It could be a suite parlor or even a traditional room that has a built in hide-away bed. (Today's options are nothing like the old "Murphy" beds – today's choices include affordable, designer approved models, complete with bookcases and artwork incorporated within a cabinet).

If there is absolutely no space anywhere in your hotel, you can still partner with someone adjacent to your business. Many of today's restaurant chains, ranging from Olive Gardens to family style restaurants like Shoneys', have separate portions of their stores that can meet and feed 10-50 people.

Now that you have a place to hold a meeting, how do you find these potential clients?

The list is extensive and many are in your existing base of contacts. They include your suppliers, your trade organizations, your social networks and local service clubs like Rotary Club or Lions.

Your staff is another base for referrals. They all belong to churches, PTA type organizations, social or garden clubs, sporting leagues, etc. These groups need to be able to plan their upcoming events, house outside speakers and meet for a wide range of reasons. There is no reason your hotel cannot be the meeting spot.

It takes some thought, looking at under-utilized space and discussion with your network of contacts. The payoff is worth it.

Common Sense Thoughts
on
Strategies to Make You
Successful in Hotel Sales

◆ ◆ ◆ ◆ ◆

There really is no such thing as out-standing individual sales performance in the hospitality world.......continuing successful sales are the results of total team effort by the entire staff

—Harry Mullikin, retired President, Western International (WESTIN) Hotels

(quote found in Educational Institute's Hospitality for Sale)

◆ ◆ ◆ ◆ ◆

Chapter 12

Understanding the Role of Sales

Accountability does not happen automatically – it usually requires the personal involvement and commitment of the general manager to get everyone to be part of the effort.

In a purely accounting sense, the sales department is classified as an expense (Advertising and Promotion), as are departments relating to engineering, energy and the general manager. While engineering and energy are services that support the needs of the guests, sales (and at least some general managers) is an area that more accurately is a legitimate revenue producer.

It is not the intent here to discuss with the accountants how to code line items, but rather to recognize that revenues and sales bookings do not occur only because of a brand or a location. While some guests stay at your hotel for one of those reasons, many more rooms are occupied and more guests are satisfied because someone took the responsibility and time to personally carry the "sales" message to potential clients.

Craig Moon, former GM at an older airport Holiday Inn in Memphis, Tennessee in the early 1990s, used to print the following on everyone's business cards:

Name of the individual

Official Title, such as Executive Housekeeper

And then under the official title would be the word
SALES

What was the effect of that single word?

Craig said it almost always generated comments from suppliers or other people who came in contact with his traditional operational staff. While Memphis was once the headquarters city for Holiday Inns, his team recognized that everyone had to be thinking of sales. Almost everyone who actually read this team's business cards would be inclined to ask the housekeeper or engineer or accounting manager why the word SALES was on the card. It opened the door for the hotel staff member to reply about the team goal (everyone sells) and to ask about potential hotel and service needs.

In downtown Nashville in the late 1980s, the general manager of the 700 room Stouffers' (now Renaissance) Hotel faced the challenge of opening the 2nd largest hotel in the state in a down market. The Stouffers also was competing with one of the best-managed and marketed hotels in the nation, the Opryland Hotel (then 1,200 rooms) that had a better location. John Bruns, the GM mentioned above, was not dismayed by the challenge. A natural optimist, Bruns began a practice of every day involvement with his sales team.

While he did not micro-manage the process, he attended the daily sales meetings (7:30 am and 5 PM) to offer support, suggestions and, at times, direction. Bruns successor, Bill Otto, followed a similar course and over the next 4 years, the hotel found a niche of it own that allowed it to be successful. Both moved to additional career challenges: Bruns in development and management at Ritz- Carlton and Otto as chief operating officer for Marcus Hotels.

Recognizing that someone needs to accept the challenge of the daily action plans is part of the battle; it is the execution of them that wins it.

Chapter 13

New Year's Resolutions

You say, this is not New Year's – this is the middle of the year. The calendar may say July, but think back to how you have been conducting your sales efforts this year, be it February or November. Did you create a usable, effective sales and marketing plan THIS year?

If you did – congratulations !

If you didn't, well, read on anyway.

Now comes the hard question – did you follow the sales action steps you felt were appropriate when you made the plan? You know the answer – most of us do not follow either personal or business resolutions unless we build in a reminder system. That system can be using key result areas or personal business objectives that we track and formally review with someone else monthly or quarterly. It may include submitting monthly reports on actual compared to plan in bookings, calls, trips, etc.

Regardless of the month, think about TODAY committing yourself to a fresh start. Once again, resolve a new effort. Some ideas we feel have solid and proven value include:

1. Sell Price Last: It's really the least important selling point of all. People want value, but if you know where you are competition-wise, price should not be the breaking point if you are competitive.

2. Cut Down On Giveaways: Comp rooms, free parking, free A/V and various other "freebies" are not always necessary ingredients in closing a deal; "listen" to what the potential client feels is important to them.

3. Close As Soon As Possible: The prospect you leave behind may be closed by the competition. Time is important to everyone, so use yours effectively.

4. Increase the Number of Your Sales Calls: If you make more calls, you meet more prospects; if you meet more prospects, you can do more selling, and if you do more selling, you close more sales. (The law of averages works.)

5. Have Sincere Pride in Your Product and Service: Be proud of where you work; then, where you work will be proud of you.

6. Be Persistent: Most sales are closed after the fourth or fifth call.

7. Be Loyal: One of the greatest virtues of selling is loyalty to your hotel, your manager and your owner.

8. Ask For the Business: Too many salespeople are on Public Relations calls; they forget to ask for the order.

9. Communicate More: Let the staff (especially the switchboard and front office) know where you are and where you're going to be.

10. Have Confidence in Yourself and Your Team: The sellers confidence in the product results in the potential buyer's confidence, more often than not, results in a sale.

11. Be Nice: Training people to be nice is tough, so only hire nice people.

12. Find Your Balance Between Aggressive and Assertive Selling: Sales isn't a fistfight. Find a happy medium between high and low pressure sales techniques. In fact, a confident professional does not need pressure to close a sale, but rather assists the potential client in solving their needs. Think of the way Saturn Automobiles are sold. No negotiation off sticker price – what the company feels a fair value, a knowledgeable sales professional who listens and a good product/service.

13. Keep In Touch Regularly: Don't lose contact with a prospect. Phone calls, notes, newsletters, even birthday cards, are good ways to remind people that you're still interested in them.

14. Don't Criticize: Sell your features against the competition's, but don't stoop to criticism. Take the high road.

15. Be a Self-Starter: Don't wait for your manager or your home office to" wind you up" every day.

16. Be Honest: Don't sell what you don't have, and be honest about your hotel's facilities.

17. Keep Your Word: Whatever you promise, you must deliver. In fact, over-deliver on personal attention and service.

18. Talk and Deliver Quality: Quality is what people want these days. Whether it's the quality of your hotel's services, its food or its staff- quality sells!

19. Write it Down: Reconfirm, in writing, everything upon which you and your prospect have agreed

20. Be Enthusiastic!: Nothing's as contagious as enthusiasm, whether it's with your staff or a client.

21. Educate Yourself Continuously: Keep learning as much as you can about our business. There are too many salespeople out there who don't know enough about hotel operations.

22. Don't Gripe About Work: If you're unhappy with your job or your boss, straighten it out. Or quit.

23. Do Not Use Canned Pitches: Yes, you need to practice your presentation but canned pitches appear to be rehearsed and frequently less than truthful, so don't use them to sell your hotel. Know your product. Be convincing in a normal, conversational manner.

24. Forget the Word "can't": You "can't" a person to death or your negativity may cause them to book elsewhere. Say, "Yes, we can" instead, assuming of course that you can deliver. You're part of a team, so keep "can't" out of your conversation and correspondence.

25. Use Action Calendars: They're needed to plan the work ahead, and they allow you to adjust your schedule as necessary.

26. Dress the Part: Don't go overboard on clothes styles. The classic look is still the best for sales.

27. Be a Joiner: Be active in your community; join professional groups like MPI, HSMAI or your local hospitality associations.

28. Talk to Your Manager or Owner Regularly: Keep him or her advised of what's going on daily; it'll improve communications and productivity.

There is nothing magic about the 28 points above, except that they do work. Why 28? The best answer we can say is we didn't want to have too many or too few. Add your own success factors, but follow those that work for you.

The economy will always be up in some parts of the world and down in others. Today, oil and energy is hot, next year it may be textiles and the year after dot.coms may make a comeback.

Ask those people you admire if they work from a set of goals. You already know the answer – seriously working resolutions regularly pays off.

Chapter 14

Everyone Should Know
What the Sales Department Does

We all want to be treated like a VIP – it is in our nature. When we think of a favorite restaurant, most of us will likely recall a place where the food is good, the value is fair and the service is memorable. We like to go to a place where they use our name (remember the theme song from CHEERS?) and where we are made to feel "special."

Guests choose hotels in a similar fashion. They choose a specific hotel because it was great the last time they were there or they choose a brand because of consistency and they feel truly welcomed.

It may be the primary responsibility of a sales manager or perhaps general manager to "sell" in a formal method the services of a hotel, but the entire staff must know what is involved.

The entire staff must know what was promised to a guest, whether it is a group meeting staying for a week using meeting space and banquets or an individual guest staying only overnight.

While this sounds elementary, there are so many unnecessary problems that hotel staff and guests face because of the lack of effective communication. Hotel owners and managers need a strong sense of priority to honor the commitments made by the sales team. If that guest is satisfied with the ways the hotel has met its' commitments (ranging from parking to group blocks to extending check-out), then the hotel manager or sales person now has an excellent opportunity to get a repeat booking immediately. For this to happen, though, the operation team must communicate what happened during the guests' stay- good, bad or ugly.

Effective and complete communication between sales and operations is essential for long-term success. This means that the GM or sales team should meet at least quarterly with operational departments. These meetings need not be long – under 30 minutes – but should include the following with line staff, such as cooks, wait staff, housekeepers, desk staff, accounting, engineers, etc.;

1. How groups and individuals book at the hotel

2. How much time and effort it takes to get groups

3. How future and repeat business depends on service

4. How the operations staff's responsiveness is essential to total guest satisfaction (remembering the indifference factor discussed in the last chapter)

5. .How the market is competitive

6. How each staff member makes a difference in sales and service

Improved compensation and benefits depend on profitability and satisfied guests. The sales team has to "sell" internally to the rest Of the hotel staff as well as to potential guests.

Chapter 15

Smaller Properties Have a Distinct Need for Sales and Marketing Plan

There is no question about the fact that more hotels are being built each year. While the rate of construction varies by market and location, competition is still growing almost everywhere. Not many hotels are being converted into other uses these days nor are many closing their doors. Add all this together and one finds that the pressure to find and keep customers continues to grow.

When you add the franchise and royalty fees associated with many franchised brands, the financial cost of success (and in some markets survival) can appear staggering to smaller (under 100 rooms) hotels and inns.

Managers and owners of smaller properties must look at time and effort as a realistic cost of reaching success in their hotels. Because many smaller hotels do not have a full-time (or even part time) sales person, the owner or GM must undertake that responsibility. Leaving it to the "brand" alone is not sufficient, as too many brands are controlled by a very small number of holding or franchise companies and their brands are often competing with each other in the same market.

Managers and owners must identify meaningful market research, determine avenues for effective public relations and promotions and still find the time for direct sales.

To do the job well, an old saying rears its head: "You must work the plan." To accomplish that however, means there must be a plan to work.

A basic plan can identify the kinds of business segments the hotel currently has, such as business, youth groups, tours, vacationers, truckers, etc. The plan also considers which kind would be the most logical and profitable in the future.

Once the markets that are accessible are identified, the strategy can be developed to promote those market segments that are meaningful from a volume (occupancy) and profit perspective.

Some hotels hire college students or mothers seeking part time employment while their children are in school. These options can be very cost effective and there are success stories in virtually every brand and region of North America.

The best ways for managers/owners to get more business is to become active in local community activities AND to make a certain number of sales calls by phone and in person daily. Involvement in local activities gives one the reputation on being the local hotelier or go-to person. It may require some volunteer work on committees or public service projects, but your interest is in that community.

If a manager/owner will commit enough time to make 5 to 10 calls per day, that would equal up to between 250 and 500 personal contacts per year. This personal networking, while cost effective, should likely yield substantial business.

Unfortunately, the management/ownership at many smaller hotels become so involved in operations that they end up working the desk or in the restaurant so frequently that they seldom have time for community involvement or sales. Too many people decide to save $65 by working a shift and don't recognize the long-term effects of not competing in the marketing and selling arena.

Effective operators of smaller properties will dedicate at least 25% of their time (week-day, prime contact hours) to networking and selling. Hoteliers who do not either handle this critical responsibility themselves or insure that it is handled by someone competent run the risk of their investment failing. It is an unnecessary failure.

"Your education won't end when your school days are over unless you are intent on becoming obsolete"

—Wes Roberts, in <u>*Straight A's Never Made*</u>
<u>*Anybody Rich*</u>

Chapter 16

Marketing Plans Cannot Sit on Shelves

One of the hardest things to do in a hotel is to turns goals into reality. Too often, those goals may be thought of and discussed, but not written down or acted on. When they are written down, it is as a memo or the introduction to a marketing plan, but with no or inadequate plans to make those goals become reality.

Hotel owners, managers and sales managers at every size hotel and brand share the goal of satisfying guests. Many have ideas on how to accomplish that profitably, but do not create the road map on how to convert those goals into fact. Without a workable, measurable plan, the hotel will likely fail to reach its true potential.

Budgets are created to provide a projection of income and expenses so there are "no unexpected surprises." Marketing plans are created to make sure that there is a "plan" to meet those budgets, yet all of us have all seen detailed plans that sit on a shelf somewhere for up to several months at a time. Someone may then decide to "see where we are in the plan," but usually at that point some of those "unpleasant, unexpected surprises" have already been discovered. If business levels are acceptable, the plan may be declared a winner, and stay on the shelf until time to plan next year. If business is poor, the previous manager is too often blamed for inadequate planning and no further discussion is held on the execution of the plan.

Sales plans, marketing plans and financial budgets all require regular attention, monitoring and tweaking. While all may forecast twelve months of anticipated volumes and activities, the market changes almost monthly and someone must review, respond and follow-up to those changes.

Below are the most important steps to make marketing and sales plans work:

1. Those responsible for the plans should be involved in making it. Getting people to buy into a plan is much easier if they helped create it. Owners and managers obviously have final approvals.

2. Goals should be attainable. Unrealistic goals will make people give up before they try. Goals that are too easy defeat the purpose of the plan.

3. Goals should be specific and include time frames. For example, X number of sales calls per week, attending Y trade shows attended in the appropriate month, etc.

4. Goals should have specific methods for reaching them, such as personal visits, working old files, follow-up calls on outside leads, etc.

5. Action plans and steps are the heart of any successfully implemented marketing plan. This means each person has particular assignments to complete by certain dates. This can be finalizing advertising for Valentine's Day promotions, contacting all the athletic director's office of visiting sports teams for the local college (by sport) by month, the dates planned to participate in sales blitzes with other hotels of the same brand, etc.

6. Once the actions steps are reviewed and approved by the manager or owner, a follow-up system needs to be implemented. Each month, the action steps need to be individually reviewed. In larger hotels, several people may complete that. In smaller hotels with the GM frequently assuming at least some of the sales activities, it means setting a specific time (the first Tuesday of each month at 4:30 PM for example) to update the action steps planned were met and to decide if options need to be considered for the current month.

7. Goals must be measurable. You cannot change the economy, but your actions can change how your hotel fares. When reviewing the financial numbers monthly, it is relatively easy to compare revenues or profits with budget or last year. With sales actions steps, it still requires comparing results with the plan. This means matching sales calls planned with those completed, examining participation in brand programs, etc.

8. Staff performance appraisals must be done regularly, and ideally quarterly. This does not suggest quarterly financial reviews, but giving regular and formal "report cards" to staff. We all like to know how we are doing and waiting for an annual report is usually too long and what might have been easily corrected in April has become a bad and regular habit by November. When the financial review does come, connecting the sales actions completed to the plan makes logical financial sense because the results are usually apparent.

Marketing and sales plans are only effective if managers, owners and sales staff view the process as living and important. Regular reviews of tactics that do and do not work are essential to long-term success.

"When someone buys, they want to feel they have something special. People will buy anything that's one to a customer."

—Sinclair Lewis

♦ ♦ ♦ ♦ ♦

Chapter 17

Using Your Business Card as an Effective Sales Tool

If you think back on your career, a major step was when you were entitled to your first business card. That "entitlement" was sort of a rite of passage – a sign of having "made it." Chances are that you gave that card to as many people as you could – at least for a while. As time wore on, you didn't have to re-print as many as the first year. Other things took priority.

Well, we have found that business cards are one of the most under-utilized sales tools in the hospitality industry by many people.

Today, successful hoteliers, sales managers, general managers and owners value this low-cost, easy-to-carry, easy-to distribute sales piece as one of their most valuable tools. Prior to the 1990s, most of them were fairly basic – name, title, company name and address, phone number and perhaps the company slogan or motto.

Today's cards contain much more information and include the above basics, proper brand identity if you belong to a referral group or franchise, as well as fax number, email and web site address. Some cards include a cell or home phone number if you have the kind of position or personality that is service sensitive enough to warrant the kind of commitments that tell existing and POTENTIAL customers that you care MORE than your competition. (Yes, we have a bias here regarding service.)

Today's cards may be dual or tri-fold in design, listing your property's facilities in some detail. The number of rooms, banquet or meeting capacity, special services, saunas, spas, casinos or recreational facilities may be listed.

Some cards include amenities such as managers' receptions or continental breakfast. Some include simple maps to explain awkward accesses, confusing street addresses or exit directions from nearby interstate highways. Other features may be four-color photographs of the hotel or perhaps the view from the hotel's front door. The decision is yours on content, but your local printer, hotel association or franchise director can give you a wealth of options that have been successful for others.

After the cards are printed, what's next?

The next is the fun AND critical part of using them effectively: distribution. Following are some distribution ideas we have seen used at hotels throughout the world:

1. As an introduction to almost everyone you meet for the first time. One never knows when they might need lodging/meeting/food services in your area.

2. In all correspondence. Everyone has some kind of Rolodex.

3. In all billing. A thank you on the back of your card can promote great goodwill!

4. In all payments. Your suppliers also need lodging/meeting/food services in your area at some point. We must all learn to regularly ASK FOR THE SALE! And that includes those from whom we buy.

5. At all industry and business meetings. We all need to network.

6. In your restaurant. If you meet and greet guests, as either the GM or any one in public contact. Let them know you care about them.

7. At check-in/out. A brochure or business card rack at the desk works for some hotels, but a manager on duty or GM personally thanking EXISTING guests at checkout and asking them to return impresses many travelers. Giving business cards is a reminder of the experience that they might relate to others back home and carries great referral potential.

8 For complimentary or discounting purposes when appropriate.

9. With all sales and marketing promotional pieces. Put a name with the hotel.

10. As a thank-you. A personal note on the back of your business card communicates an individualized sign of appreciation.

Business cards today can cost as little as five to ten cents each. Giving 10 out per business day equals roughly 50 per week, 200 per month and 5,000 per year. Do most members of your staff have their own business cards? Think of the multiplier effect of several people personally delivering the message of your hotel.

Can you think of any other personally delivered message that exists for under $500 a year?

◆　◆　◆　◆　◆

It Isn't Easy To Be in Sales.

"An ideal salesperson has the curiosity of a cat, the tenacity of a bulldog, the friendship of a little child, the diplomacy of a wayward husband, the patience of a self-sacrificing wife, the enthusiasm of a Sinatra fan, the assurance of a Harvard man, the good humor of a comedian, the simplicity of a jack-ass, and the tireless energy of a bill collector."

-Harry Moock, former vice president, Chrysler

◆　◆　◆　◆　◆

Chapter 18

The Power of Breakfast

The term "power breakfast" was a very popular term in the late 1980s and early 1990s. It was frequently used to describe all the "deals" that sophisticated and influential people were able to close business agreements in previously under-utilized hours.

It makes sense that a hotel, as a combination of a product and a service, is easier to sell in a face-to-face situation. The best chance for sales people to close may very well be when the potential client can see first-hand what a good experience their guests will receive.

Most hotel sales people will agree that group business, meetings and contract sales are usually closed when the prospect client has had a first hand opportunity to see the property "in action." While some clients include an overnight as part of the due diligence review, many others cannot compare the full benefits of a rooms only hotel in competition with full service properties.

Breakfast at both rooms-only and full service hotels is a chance to shine, as more salespeople than ever are viewing breakfast as an ideal time to "do" business.

Inviting potential clients for breakfast and a tour of the hotel appears to be most appealing to both hoteliers and buyers. Here are a few reasons why business breakfasts make sense for everyone:

1. There are fewer cancellations for breakfast appointments, mainly because the invitee hasn't had the problem of getting "tied up" at the office.

2. Doing business at breakfast allows the invitee to get back to the office early and get in a full day.

3. The hotel salespeople have more productive time available because they cut down on waiting time for their invitee and on travel time

4. Time spent at breakfast is viewed by many as more productive than other meals, because all participants view this as a time for productive business for all parties. There is less likely to be quite as much warm-up banter, as everyone wants to get down to business.

5. The question of "to drink or not to drink" doesn't need to be addressed and avoids the sensitive issue of alcohol before the meal.

6. Breakfast at full service restaurants is still a best value, when compared to other meals.

7. Both parties have cleared minds first thing in the morning and decisions can usually be made quicker.

8. Hotel restaurants are almost always busier at breakfast than at any other meal. Doesn't it make sense to show a restaurant that appears to be well used and popular?

9. Having the invitee to breakfast should insure a tour of the hotel if you are dining at your place. Select a nearby place if your hotel does not offer Breakfast so the tour can take place.

10. The hotel staff will also likely be fresh and more alert in the morning, providing a positive service impression.

Many room's only properties offer very attractive continental breakfasts. Your potential client will likely be positively impressed with your presentation that will be part of their guests' stay.

McDonalds' restaurants discovered the value of breakfast and turned formerly closed hours into periods of substantial profitability by meeting the needs of people who were looking for a quick, perceived value option for breakfast. For many McDonalds in the US and Canada, this has become their highest volume period. Perhaps it is time for hoteliers to follow this lead and increase the volume of "power" used at breakfast.

♦ ♦ ♦ ♦ ♦

You'll make more sales if you remember what management expert Peter Drucker said: "There are no dumb customers."

♦ ♦ ♦ ♦ ♦

Common Sense Thoughts
on
Making Your
Sales Efforts Work

Don't go after a friend to make a sale - go after a sale to make a friend

—Adrian Philips, long time Executive Vice President, Hotel Sales Management Association International

(quote found in Educational Institute's Hospitality for Sale)

◆ ◆ ◆ ◆ ◆

Chapter 19

Sales Leadership Techniques. . . "ing" Is Actually a Verb.

Ask any US history buff and they will tell you that Jimmy Carter is probably one of the two most intelligent men ever to serve as US President. (The other by the way was probably Thomas Jefferson.) Regardless of your political leanings, there are few of us that believe that Carter did not work harder than Carter's successor, Ronald Reagan, yet history will likely record Reagan's terms as accomplishing significantly more. Carter tried "managing" the system, often taking home 300 pages of nightly reading. Reagan's preference to "leading" people worked for his temperament and he seldom worked after seven in the evening, according to his presidential library memoirs.

Effective sales efforts in hotels in this new century require several "ings" from dedicated general managers and sales representatives. These include:

1. Plann-*ing*: the business plan, marketing plan and sales action plan are all essential tools in today's successful hotels.

2. Organiz-*ing*: creating a balanced sales/operational team, setting standards, accountability and providing the structures for success need to come early and be regularly valued.

3. Direct-*ing*: daily interest is essential.

4. Controll-*ing*: measuring results are all critical; the GM has the right to information re: results, problems and possible solutions.

5. Motivat-*ing*: this is another word for "coach-ing". It varies with the individual, but we all need feedback, support and constructive criticism.

6. Communicat-*ing*: two-way discussions on the good, bad and ugly can make the bad and ugly go away.

7. Train-*ing*: continuing education isn't only for GMs or department heads; everyone needs both focused and general opportunities for self-improvement

8. Listen-*ing*: a most difficult task for most of us, as we tend to want to be tell-ing our story. General managers, owners and sales staffs need to remember to have realistic growth goals for the hotel and the staff that can do the "sell-ing" to get everyone there!

**Lead, rather than manage, your sales effort
for effective results.**

Chapter 20

Sales Leadership Techniques ...ing Is Actually a Verb. (Part 2)

"Meet-ing" your commitments"

The *"ings"* lessons we shared in the last chapter led us to the sequel of identifying challenges in properly servic-ing meetings.

Obstacle to Success

Verbal commitments lead to many times planners are "told" what the hotel will provide, but the promise is not communicated.

Resolution

Put all commitments in writing, and get confirmation from the planner or booker.

Obstacle to Success

Meeting room set-ups are not what were expected.

Resolution

All parties need to know exact capabilities. Hotel staff should draw up all possible variations and keep trying variations for continual improvement.

Obstacle to Success

Food service is not what was expected.

Resolution

As not all hotels feature in-house food service, outside caterers and/or inside service must have a clear understanding of the goals of the meetings. The chef, F&B manager or restaurant lessee should meet   with planners to insure satisfaction.

Obstacle to Success

'What you told me, you sold me."

Resolution

Make sure the charges for all room types, banquet charges (including tax and gratuities), audio visual services, meeting room charges, etc. are outlined in detail in writing in advance.

Obstacle to Success

Whom do I have to talk with now?

Resolution

Dick Scott, formerly with Hilton Hotels sales, used to team up people in sales. Each outside sales person would be kept up-to-date with someone who was almost always on property. If there was a local inquiry while the outside sales person was not in the office but in the field, the inside contact would pass the information along and the outside person would be able to show up on the local caller's doorstep, usually within hours. This is an impressive response technique. With cell phones and virtual 100% accessibility today, this is even easier and faster.

Obstacle to Success

Accounting snafus

Resolution

While it may be easy or even fashionable to beat or pick on the "bean- counters", it is often accounting that is the last contact a guest may have   with your hotel. If the billing is not accurate, re-booking what   may have been a great experience may not come as readily as it should.

The written details of the meeting should include who pays for what incidentals, for rooms, for meals, etc. Cash flow will be much smoother with a clean, detailed and accurate billing.

◆　◆　◆　◆　◆

The best product must be sold. People won't come to you and take it away from you. You must go to them."

—*Edna Newman*

◆　◆　◆　◆　◆

Chapter 21

Employing This Proven Formula Should Give Boost To Sales Activity

Many areas of the country have been hit with over-development of hotels creating more of a supply of rooms than what is needed. The most recent cycle has been a range of extended stay products, which was preceded by what some call "hard" budget properties. There will always be a cycle and as salespeople, we need to recognize the strengths of our brand and property styles to compete effectively.

Some areas have been affected with an economic situation that has created a decline in room demand in at least some market segments. Both of these types of situations have created volume problems for hotels that adversely affect the bottom line of a profit and loss statement. There is a desperate need for additional sales at locations that have this problem.

Some hoteliers, in the interest of showing good performance, start by making cuts in service and sales, when the answer to the problem really lies in improving sales performance by getting a better share of the available business in the market area. It may even mean an increase in the sales budget— adding some or more sales people — if that will work to improve productivity.

The Feiertag 10-Percent Formula is a very basic system that we have tested at selected hotel properties and have found to work. The statistics show that 10 percent of selected sales activity will result in definite business immediately.

If you are serious about booking business quickly, we ask you to put this formula to the test and we think you'll be sending us a letter or an email detailing your successes.

Here's how it works.

• **Cold Calls:** Take two full days devoted to cold calling only, making at least 30 calls (more is better). Call only on companies whose business you've never had before. Don't make prearranged appointments— no phone calls, but rather all cold calls outside and in person. We'll bet 10 percent of the calls will result in definite bookings, while at least another 10 percent will be excellent leads for future bookings.

• **Files:** Review: Take two full days devoted to examining and following up on old existing files. Review and work at least 30 files. Call the contact on each old file and attempt to book some kind of business. Invite the contact in for a tour of your facilities. Just start at the beginning of any file drawer and pull the first 80 that are not due to come up on the trace system in a short period of time. Here the focus should be on files that have not been worked for a long period of time. Again, 10 percent of all files worked should result in some type of confirmed business,

• **Wedding Receptions:** Using the newspaper society section or other source for wedding reception leads (via engagement announcements), call 30 prospects for wedding receptions and invite them (bride-to-be, parents, prospective groom) over to show your property and sample your food. At least 10 percent should book with you.

• **Existing Room Accounts:** Many times, companies that are already supplying overnight room business are overlooked as meeting-business prospects. Telephone or visit 30 of the current room business accounts. Find out who makes decisions on meeting locations and sell them on using your meeting facilities. At least 10 percent of the calls will result in definite bookings.

• **Legitimate Proposals:** Send out at least 30 proposals to prospects (not covered in the four categories listed) with whom you are already working and who have shown interest in your property. Much more than 10 percent of the proposals will result in definite bookings.

Having a positive attitude about doing business in a distressed situation will result in productive sales activity. Following the basics will result in solid business and we challenge you to take this test and report the results back to us.

◆ ◆ ◆ ◆ ◆

Some observations on preparation:
"If you don't do your homework, you
won't make your free throws"

—*Boston Celtics star Larry Bird*

◆ ◆ ◆ ◆ ◆

Chapter 22

A Blueprint For Bigger
Payoffs From Your Sales Efforts

Would you like to make your sales effort more successful? Follow these guidelines when soliciting and booking business and servicing accounts:

Acquire and use good marketing knowledge. Finding out who your customers are, where they are coming from, how they came to select your property, why they stay at your property, how long they stay and how much they spend— among other information —will help focus your sales effort.

1. **Plan A Good Market Mix.** The mix of business reflects how much of what type of business you're doing. Ask yourself: What percentage of my total room sales comes from meetings, transient business and other categories? What mix of business would be most profitable?

2. **Know Your Competition and specifically your direct competitors.** Having a thorough knowledge of the other properties near you can help you size up your property and determine the areas in which you can compete the best, whether it is location, price, size, product, service or amenities. The idea, of course, is to sell your positives.

3. **Question Your Multiple Price Policy.** There's nothing wrong with selective discounting. Hotels have been doing it for years, with special off-season, corporate, group, senior citizen and military rates, among others. But which special rates are generating business for you? A periodic review of all your rates will help you establish the multiple-rate policy that's right for you. If you make the decision to work with a discounter such as PriceLine, Travelocity or the new "hot" service, track your actual demand (rooms used, rooms denied because you were

full, rooms declined for reasons of rate, location, etc.) so you can evaluate intelligently the business decision.

4. Make Good Business Contacts And Make Them Work For You. Getting good business contacts is the first step, and making sure they're bringing business into your property the second. Make sure your contacts are frequent users of your property and then ask them to provide you leads.

5. Try New Things. Remember: most successful entrepreneurs would not be where they are today if they didn't take a chance and try new things. Come up with new ideas to promote business and don't be afraid to put them into action. Develop new sales techniques to book more rooms and new proposals to land more group business. If only half of your new schemes works, you'll be ahead of the game.

6. Be Attentive To Costs. In any business, spending more than you take in, of course, is dangerous. Cost effectiveness in selling for a hotel is very important. As total sales expenditures start to creep up, you must continue to expect a greater return from your sales effort. Budgeting for sales and monitoring the sales budget against results are two big musts.

7. Follow Good Management Procedures. In general, try to do a better job communicating, developing , training, motivating, planning, organizing, directing and controlling. It's not enough these days to hire a salesperson and say: "Get out there and sell."

8. Recruit High-Quality People. You want salespeople who are sincere, believable, down-to-earth, friendly, well dressed and well mannered; in other words, folks who will represent your property well.

9. Set Realistic Growth Plans. Assess where you are today and decide where you want to be next year, the year after, and so on.

10. Sell Aggressively. Aggressive sales- people are the ones who book the business. You can be aggressive while still being friendly, credible and sincere. Being tenacious, following up, ensuring customer confidence all these add up to aggressiveness.

◆ ◆ ◆ ◆ ◆

Not every customer will buy. If you have a good product and service, someday they will come around if you don't give up. For example, Coca-Cola sold only four hundred sodas its first year. Sometimes it takes time for a new product to develop a following.

McGraw-Hill estimates it takes an average of $5\frac{1}{2}$ visits before a customer says, "yes" to a major sale.

◆ ◆ ◆ ◆ ◆

Chapter 23

"It's a Wonderful Day in the Neighborhood": Hometown Business

This opening line from a long running children's' program in the US – Mr. Rogers – actually can be used to symbolize the foundations of our sales efforts. The foundation, of course, is the very base of any building.

The guests who stay in your hotels come from literally all over the world. Regardless of the location of your hotel, the world is getting "smaller" with more people traveling globally.

Our question is this - how necessary is it to take those sales trips all over the US and Canada (or beyond)? Industry estimates are, that for the typical hotel/inn, more than 50% and in many cases up to 80% of all rooms business probably is referred or comes from their own "neighborhood."

Unless a hotel is located in a national park or in an extremely rural location (like many resorts), someone at your hotel should be able to generate a substantial amount of business through local contacts. Regularly calling on those local contacts, asking the right questions, qualifying, following-up, inviting them to see your property or to stay as your guest (on a comp basis) should translate those qualifying or cold calls to prospects with needs to confirm business.

As with small meetings, most local companies generate some overnight business travelers. Most local business people belong to some kind of organizations, ranging from trade or professional associations, service or fraternal clubs, social or religious groups. Getting these people to give your hotel a chance locally can lead to satisfied, repeat customers which then frequently lead to referrals outside their immediate companies by word-of-mouth.

Think of all the businesses with which your hotel interacts – banks, food suppliers, plumbers, electricians, pool supply firms, law firms, the newspaper, radio stations, landscape companies, etc. Now think of all the extra contacts you and your staff have, by daily contact with other community services, such as schools, libraries, police/fire departments, government offices, nursing homes, grocery stores, retail locations............ the list is very extensive.

Creating a logical, manageable action plan for contacting the above local services will provide an even larger network of referrals and potential guests who can easily become regular guests at your hotel. It does require thought, some brainstorming with your team and some face-to-face time outside of your hotel, but the payoff is there.

Chapter 24

Who Would Like to Have an Additional 10 Sales People at Virtually No Cost?

What about 20 more? 50? 75?

If your hotel belongs to a membership, referral or franchise group, there is a large, well-trained group of professionals who are already on the payroll of the organization. They are motivated, interested but too often not well versed enough in the details of your hotel.

The solution will cost your hotel some travel and promotional dollars, but the payback is worth it. Presentations at reservations centers are opportunities for one on one educational sessions with the reservationists who handle the calls that go into the central reservations offices.

Many of these offices are located in the United States and Canada and handle hundreds of thousands of calls annually. Obviously those calls are not for only one or two hotels, and the reservationists relay the information on their computer screens to inquiring guests.

There remains something impersonal about computers though. In spite of their technological superiority, computers can only relay technical information and it is the skill of the reservationists who often makes the sale for your hotel.

Presentations are handled differently at different centers, but most provide a forum to allow hotel sales staff to educate the agents on the unique characteristics of their hotel. Some hoteliers provide refreshments and snacks, while others rely on videos, give-aways, promotions and attention grabbers to provide an incentive for agents to attend their programs.

Agents have a choice to take their breaks in your forum or in their break room. It is left to your creativity and enthusiasm to encourage them to choose to become more aware of your hotel's special features.

Check with your brand's reservations centers and find out how to add a small army of sales professionals to your team. You'll find it a very smart decision.

Chapter 25

Extending Your Sales Team
or
Make Travel Agents A Regular Part of Your Sales Programs

The travel agent, whether part of an international con-glomerate or a small town independent, should be treated as part of your sales team. The truth is, they cost comparatively little (equal in most cases to the equivalent of a 10% discount), and have access to clients you may have no way of ever reaching.

Once thought to be only for the leisure or the vacation traveler, today's agent handles a wide array of arrangements for business, leisure and group markets. Recent surveys show that more than 500,000 US based companies and most Federal government agencies use travel agencies to handle their needs. Agents are always trying to find the best value airfare options and lodging arrangements to fulfill individual travel, meetings and conferences needs.

Group incentive travel is another important area for today's agent. Finding the right product/service/location as the right "reward" means that agents today have to be made aware of new benefits that your hotel offers.

For every business, repeat customers are critical to long-term success. For hoteliers, repeat business comes many times from travel agents. The agent's incentives include satisfied clients, competitive value (price, services, frequent traveler recognition including airline or hotel bonus programs) and commissions promptly paid.

While agencies may be levying service charges to their clients for airline or hotel services, earned commissions remain an important part of their revenue stream. Traditional commissions are 10%, although some hotels have successfully used higher figures during certain critical low demand periods to get agency attention and some business from primarily leisure travelers who may be open to suggestions on optional destinations.

Getting the attention of agencies is a major challenge. Mailing them brochures and assuming their staff will take the time to read them in detail is like playing the lottery – there is an occasional winner, but most lottery tickets (and brochures) end up in the circular file.

Hoteliers have found some of the following approaches to be effective in reaching travel agencies:

1. Personal selling visits to individual agencies

2. Advertising in trade magazines and directories aimed at audiences of targeted agencies.

3. Packaging their hotel with other services, especially for the leisure market as part of a destination. This can include food, admission to some area attractions, and auto rental for a day, etc.

4. Working with their State/Provincial Tourism Office, Convention and Visitors Bureau or Chamber of Commerce in all promotional efforts involving travel agencies.

5. Participating in brand sponsored agency promotional activities, including advertising and personal selling events.

6. Offering qualified agents familiarization visits (no or low cost accommodations in exchange for a tour of the hotel).

7. Working with other hoteliers of the same brand or management group in focused blitzes aimed raising agency awareness and referrals.

8 Participating effectively in trade shows geared to travel agencies and consortiums

9. Thank you letters and asking for more business from agencies already using your hotel

10. Commission checks mailed the same day as the guest leaves – except for those hotels using a central payment system by the brand

◆　◆　◆　◆　◆

We lose sales because we don't ask for the order. Henry Ford was once asked by an insurance agent whom he had known for many years why he never got any of Ford's business. Ford replied: "You never asked me."

◆　◆　◆　◆　◆

Chapter 26

Front Line Sales People

Too few hoteliers pay enough attention to front-line staff and their ability to sell for our hotels. People who work at your front desks, van drivers, bell staff, telephone operators, doormen, cashiers, night auditors – they are the front line for many potential guests. And "potential" is the correct word, because if those people mentioned above do not receive the proper information, knowledge and attention to meet the needs of those potential guests, many of them will likely keep on looking for other lodging options.

Jim Sullivan, a noted hospitality industry columnist and speaker, refers to the tight labor market in a different fashion than most people. Rather than facing a labor shortage problem, he maintains that what we face is really a "turnover problem." In his talks and writings, he constantly reminds us that we must recognize the individuality of our staff. While one could argue it is difficult and challenging, the options are worse. Continued, costly turnover and management spending too much time in operations hurts business potential. Reducing turnover is part of the manager's responsibility, but there is a need to balance efforts in operations and in sales. A satisfied employee usually gives better service, which makes for a satisfied guest. It makes more sense to have managers greeting and selling when there are many potential guests that are looking for a new favorite hotel in your town, but the needs of the staff are very critical to long-term success.

The makeup of our staffs varies by location, but it includes all ages, many more nationalities than ever before and tremendous ranges of interests and capabilities. The United States and Canada continue to attract immigrants from around the world who want to become citizens, but also remain attached to their original culture. Today's college freshman has a completely different perspective than those of us over age 40. Sullivan notes that those Generation Y individuals have known only one Pope. They view the Reagan years as recent to them as the Franklin Roosevelt era and have never personally felt the threat of a nuclear bomb. These new entries into our job market have always had CDs, cable TV and more choices than any generation ever in the world. It therefore makes sense that we must recognize them as the individuals they are.

A potential guest views your hotel and its' first impression only once. There is one last impression – and both of them are frequently influenced primarily by those front line jobs identified above.

How do we need to pay more attention to those people? A major part of it is attitude on the part of owners and managers. Imagine today that you are a Generation Y person, or a recent immigrant from a country 3,000 miles away. You have perhaps learned a new language, new cultural habits that are not yet comfortable, but you want to be successful.

What will either of these people think of being called or thought of as a desk "clerk?" What will they feel about the one hour of orientation or training they receive prior to assuming responsibility for a $500 bank and the second shift of a hotel that may have an asset value of $1 million, $2 million or more? Would a 66-year old, semi retired native born American or Canadian feel any different?

We must upgrade our attitudes to one that includes consistent respect, attention, reasonable fixed compensation and training so they can be successful and satisfied with their role in the hotel, as front desk sales receptionists (or whatever titles you elect). Perhaps financial incentives for 100% occupancies at agreed standards (X $ rate, no walks, etc.), for up selling to premium rooms, suites is part of the answer. Perhaps cross training, certifications or other personalized incentives may meet the needs of your staff.

Innovation must take place to improve both staff and guest satisfaction. The first greeting to a guest and a positive check-in experience can set the tone for a guest's entire stay. None of us want to speak to the top of a receptionist's head that is bowed down looking at a computer screen.

A positive first impression, a welcoming so to speak, makes the other little things that can go wrong less important. Starting the guest off negatively can set an avalanche of complaints and problems. The long-term goal is to get repeat customers, which of course adds to the most effective form of selling and marketing, word of mouth referrals.

Our front teams must be made to feel respected and important. Do your sales and management teams include them regularly in planning meetings for finding new customers and keeping existing ones? No one is closer to guests, yet so many properties ignore this resource.

The front desk team can provide tremendous leads resulting from ordinary, pleasant conversations with guests. Sales and management staff can prompt the front desk team on questions to ask.

Rewarding the desk team with recognition, incentives, promotional opportunities and respect will make an unbelievable difference in your top and bottom lines.

—

♦ ♦ ♦ ♦ ♦

*Everything comes to him who hustles
while he waits.*

—*Thomas Edison*

♦ ♦ ♦ ♦ ♦

Chapter 27

Trade Shows Can Be Invaluable If...

Success at trade shows and conferences depends on the marketing strategy you develop to sell your property and the tactics you use to turn those leads into sales calls and, eventually, bookings.

The astute salesperson will not only increase the number of sales calls at shows and conferences but also expand his prospects and personal growth over the long term.

From the standpoint of productivity, more sales calls can be made at a meeting, conference or trade show in two days than in the same amount of time on the street knocking on doors. Selecting the show or conference to attend is easy to do once you have targeted the markets you wish to reach and have completed a marketing plan.

Which groups do you want to reach?

There are gatherings for association executives, meeting planners, corporate travel managers, government individual & group travel, travel agents, wholesalers, incentive travel buyers and planners, training directors, religious conference managers, insurance conference planners and group travel producers.

If you belong to a membership, referral or franchise group, the chances are that your national and/or global sales teams are very familiar with the large shows. They may already be attending with a booth you can either buy into as a co-sponsor or join with others of your brand to make that brand stand out more than the competition. There are usually smaller chapters of all of the above groups that have trade shows regionally that can yield outstanding results because they are not as well attended by the national hotel chains.

Besides being able to attend a trade show (where contact may be made by several hundred potential buyers), there is also the chance to develop yourself, to experience new ways to conduct business and to start long-term client relationships.

Your performance at a trade show or conference is measured by how much business you are able to do at the event. You can count the number of qualified prospects and actual bookings.

It turns into a numbers game: the more contacts that are made, the more leads that can be qualified. Establish goals for yourself, such as :

• Plan to make 30 new prospect contacts the first day.

• Plan to leave the show with a specified number of qualified leads upon which to follow up.

• Plan to give out at least X of your incentive promotions or other give-aways

Making productive use of your time may mean that you will have to stay out of the "comfort zone." You may not be able to mix only with people you know because the strategy will likely not be productive. The object is to make new contacts that can provide business for your property. Too often, salespeople spend way too much time mixing with other salespeople from other properties, which is not the reason for attending the trade show.

When you select a table for group meals, look for tables occupied by potential customers. During coffee breaks, keep moving to maximize the time for new contacts.

Don't Waste Time

Spend time with prospects that can buy or are in a position to recommend or influence the buying decision. Too much time is wasted on sales presentations to persons who are not in a position to buy or have no need for a particular hotel or motel. All it takes is five to ten minutes and a few key questions to determine if you are talking to the right individual, such as:

• Ask a contact to explain how meeting sites are selected

• Find out how the prospective client recommends hotels to corporate accounts.

• Ask openly (and politely), "How do you propose I go about getting business for my hotel from your association?"

By working diligently, using probably less than 10 minutes per contact, a good salesperson could generate six to eight "cold calls" per hour or 40 new contacts in a day. Even if only 25 qualify as good leads, you are still doing well and probably far ahead of traditional cold calls to unknown clients

Using attendance listings, target those people who really need to be contacted, and, if they are not seen readily during the day, find out where they are staying and contact them there. In order to follow up on a prospect, be sure to obtain the individuals name, title, company or association, address (postal and email) and phone number. For best results, get a business card. It saves time and provides correct spellings.

Besides these vital statistics, you should also find out:

• Who else is involved in decision-making?

• What does the contact need?

• What feature of the property particularly appealed to the prospect that is what was the best benefit to them?

• What dates are being considered?

• Is this going to be a competitive bid situation, or will it be a "best for the business" decision approach?

The more information you get, the easier it will be to follow up. Then, most importantly, don't forget to follow up quickly while the contacts are fresh in everyone's mind.

Chapter 28

Sales Blitzes: A Look At the Benefits of Team Efforts

The word "blitz" does not have any synonyms in a thesaurus. The dictionary would define it as:

1. A "rash of air raid attacks"

2. A "football rush at the quarterback" or

3. A " fast and intensive campaign."

It is the third definition that matters to us. Regardless of the size (or lack of) of our sales team, it can get tired or lethargic at times. The concept of a hotel sales blitz is a remedy that brings a great deal of enthusiasm to those responsible for selling, as well as a good amount of potential business.

The hotel staff's primary involvement includes a pre-blitz orientation dinner, providing collateral material, arranging for incentive awards, and providing the service of a sales manager each evening of the blitz period. Each day, upon the return of the blitzers, the sales manager reviews each blitz call report to determine the number of calls and leads that were turned in.

And How You Can Arrange A Sales Blitz Of Your Own

A sales blitz is an intensive survey of a given geographical area to determine its market potential. The idea is to lay the groundwork for a sharp increase in business by gathering the information sales staff needs to do its job well.

The key to a successful blitz is to completely canvas an area in as little time as possible, with as few people as possible. To make that happen, proper organization is essential.

Who are The 'Blitzers'?

Anyone with a pleasant personality on a hotel's payroll can participate. Since the objective is not to sell but to gather information, the blitz team needn't be limited to members of the sales department. The idea is to extend the department's reach, not overload it with a new responsibility.

There's one critical thing to remember: the same people have to be used throughout the length of the blitz. Switching horses in midstream will only complicate matters as momentum will be lost and enthusiasm diluted.

The staff members chosen to participate have to be under the firm and direct control of one person. The director of sales is a good candidate, but that needn't be the case. The prime consideration is finding a blitz director" who can keep things under control.

The blitz director needs to start planning the operation 30 days in advance of the blitz date. Logical days to select are Tuesday, Wednesday and Thursday, when the contacts are more likely to be in town. Three days of blitzing should be the maximum. For small properties with limited amount of blitzer time available, a one or two-day blitz could be satisfactory. In fact, a one-day mini-blitz would be a good place to start experimenting with the process.

How many calls?

The answer for a full-blown blitz would likely be 30 calls a day. In six and a half hours each person should be able to conduct "30 calls" Depending on the area assigned, the number of calls will vary. In a downtown office building in a medium to large city, a higher number should be made, while in smaller or outlying industrial areas, far fewer calls could result.

After the day's calls are completed, a blitz recovery peri- od should be scheduled. It is during this time that the forms are turned in and reviewed by the blitz director or a member of the hotel's sales department. It would be appropriate to serve refreshments and snacks to the blitzers to help them unwind and discuss the day's work.

Grades are also assigned at the period when the forms are reviewed. A score chart is kept where each blitzer is credited with the number of calls and number of leads developed. Once tabulated, a daily winner of the "contest" should be announced and a prize should be awarded. After the last blitz day, a din- ner may be planned with the spouses and guests of the blitzers included in the festivities.

The real key to a successful blitz program is proper moti- vation. Management and owners need to be behind the program as much, if not more, than the participants in the program. The blitzers need to be animated and psychologically motivated throughout the program. Breakfasts with music, signs, banners, awards, and other 'mood elevators" will help bring in great results.

Since the objective of the blitz is to develop sales leads, a good deal of time and money would be wasted if a poor fol- low-up job was done. After each day's calls have been tabulat- ed, the blitz forms need to be sorted by the "grades" given each blitzer. The highest grades are obviously the forms with the best leads, and usually the ones that require immediate attention.

The sales director should determine which leads need to be followed up the very next morning and arrange the remain- ing forms in priority order for follow-up calls based on the information received.

Even while blitzers are out the next day; the sales depart- ment personnel should start on the follow-up of the previous day's work. It is important to check files first before the follow-up to see if more information on the prospect might already be available.

Although a successful blitz requires time and effort on the part of the management team, it always produces excellent results. Besides developing leads, it helps promote the property to the business community. In addition, it becomes a motivational tool for the staff members that have participated in a team effort, which creates a healthy, cooperative attitude that lasts a long time.

In organizing the calls to be made, the most helpful system is to use a city directory. The directory lists all addresses in a city by street designation. It is important to concentrate calls in one small area at a time so the blitzers aren't spread too thin.

Blitz Preparation

Index cards should be used to record the addresses of all the calls that have got to be made. These cards are then assigned to the participants based on geographical territory.

For a three-day blitz, each person may be assigned 100 calls. (A good day's work would be 30 calls per person.) Logically, in a business area of any city the calls would be located right next door to each other— or in the case of office buildings, all in the same building, with the blitzer going floor to floor.

An adequate supply of collateral material and forms are necessary. Padded blitz survey forms should be plentiful (you will need at least one per call). In addition, property brochures, fact sheets and promotional material (about the entire facility including meeting space, restaurant, lounge etc.) should be given out on each call. Low-cost "promotional or advertising" gifts may be distributed, but they're certainly not necessary.

In today's competitive market, many brands and management groups band together and "attack" an area or market believed to have potential for the brand or group of hotels. Convention and Visitors' Bureaus, Chamber of Commerce and national sales teams have had excellent success with this tactic of reaching a large number of potential clients quickly with a motivated team of interested professionals.

Always bear in mind that your own resolution to succeed is more important than any other one thing.

—*Abraham Lincoln*

Chapter 29

The Student Blitz: A Not So New Technique For Building Sales

We all know what a sales blitz is: a group of people fanning out after sales leads, making as many calls as possible in a limited area within a short span of time. Well, the 1970s introduced an effective, low-cost type of sales blitz known as "the student blitz".

Energetic college blitzers can cover a lot of ground generating sales leads by face-to-face contact. The students fill out fact or prospect survey sheets that the hotel's full-time sales staff should follow up on later. The blitzers can also "scatter" around promotional flyers on a hotel's food and beverage offerings.

There are case studies of such blitzes in major cities sponsored by major national chains stirring hundreds of firm sales leads made by as few as 10 motivated students. Immediate results totaled more than $200,000 of potential business for properties!

The sponsoring chain involved provided the students five double rooms for three nights, as well as meals, incentive awards and mileage reimbursement. An unexpected plus connected with using student blitzers is that a student can, in many instances, get in doors where an experienced salesperson may not be able to. A smiling, nervous student can disarm secretaries and executives by appealing to parental instincts or by convincing subjects that the cause of education is at stake.

131

This is not meant to sound misleading or dishonest; the truth is that these hotel or marketing majors are learning valuable lessons about what it takes to be successful in real life business.

Usually, a group of 10 people can make 1,000 calls within three days. It's important that time isn't wasted by indiscriminate running around. Calls must be planned, routes marked out, assignments made, information sheets developed, collateral material selected, briefings given and participants rehearsed. Out of 1,000 calls, typically 200-300 result in some type of sales lead. Although students are doing the legwork, it's important to have your full-time sales staff follow-up. If well planned and implemented, a student blitz can keep your employees in the hotel while outsiders drum up immediate sales leads for guest rooms, group and social business.

How do you find a marvelous resource?

It is not totally free, but can be very cost effective. One twist to student blitz programs is to engage the services of an outside source, for a fee, to handle the entire operation. This takes the administrative burden of doing a blitz away from the hotel's sales staff, thereby allowing them to continue their usual daily sales activities without taking time away from selling.

These are frequently hospitality or marketing professors at universities in your general marketplace. The professor will recruit a number of interested students for the project who may receive academic credit or fulfill a work experience requirement.

In addition to development of the leads, the amount of goodwill and promotion benefit for the hotel is virtually immeasurable. From the students' viewpoints, the experience gained by making the calls and the exposure to hotel operations could only benefit the students in their future studies and career paths. From the universities' perspective, there is "real world" connection and relevance to the marketplace, as well as the potential for obtaining business contacts and potential guest speakers.

◆ ◆ ◆ ◆ ◆

Don't talk yourself out of a sale

Mark Twain once told of the time he listened to a missionary give a sermon. Twain was terribly impressed with his religious zeal. He had real enthusiasm for his message. In fact, Twain was so impressed he decided to contribute five dollars when the collection plate was passed. Instead of stopping, the preacher kept going and going. When he finally quit, Twain was so mad that instead of making a donation, he took out a dime!

◆ ◆ ◆ ◆ ◆

Chapter 30

Principles of Profitability:
Points to Ponder

There is no single solution to the question of how to achieve profitability. There are always many variables to consider; yet certain factors need to be considered when analyzing the direction needed to increase your bottom line.

Some points to ponder when mapping a plan to improve profits are listed here. While some may seem obvious, there are a surprising number of owners, managers and companies that cling to habits that may not work as they once they did. Profit building comes from regular analysis of trends and competition, from focused planning and from some free flowing "what if we tried this...." conceptual brainstorming sessions.

Consider some of these ideas:

• **Pricing sensitivities:** – Economists, Wall Street analysts and some industry consultants predict a serious downturn in our industry. Many hotels have enjoyed several prosperous years, which were preceded by a number of very stressful and unprofitable ones. While most industries do run in some cyclical patterns, many hotels have been able to properly structure their long-term debt, which had been a primary cause of failure in the last down cycle.

• **Some markets are very price sensitive,** regardless of national economic trends. For example, a rate increase of 5% to 10% could result in a decrease of more than 5%-10% if applied at the wrong time or to the wrong market/group mix. A rate decrease of 15% might give a 15% increase in volume, but the variable costs figures (labor, energy, supplies) could significantly increase, creating a worsening profit picture. This is why ALL managers and owners need to grasp the concepts of revenue management and selective selling. There is nothing wrong with working with deep discounting services such as Travelocity or Priceline – as long as we understand our demand trends.

• **Captive Markets:** Unless you are the manager of a military-base hotel, there is no longer any such thing as a captive market. All suite hotels, extended stay properties, time-share, luxury and budget options are now available and heavily marketed to everyone regularly. Not actively marketing and caring for your traditional markets could leave you in the competitive dust.

• **Customer concentrations:** While there may be no captive markets, there are geographic and product concentrated centers. Niche marketing and positioning are critical – that's how the so called "boutique' hotels have made their impact. It still amazes us how many hotels with accessible or great locations to colleges, medical centers or airports do not have active sales efforts and programs for those centers. Yes, the state university football team may stay at an upscale, perhaps higher profile property, but there are dozens of other referral centers from that university who have very different needs, budgets or preferences.

• **Market segmentation and understanding the competition:** Some brands have confused customers with multi-brands seemingly offering comparable services at different price points. Many of us believe we know the competition – some of us measure how we are doing by comparing car counts in the parking lots at night. While this time proven habit may show the approximate number of rooms occupied, it does not adequately compare truly meaningful statistics over a one-month or year-to-date period in what counts.

• **Understanding one's competitive positioning** in RevPAR, occupancy, market penetration and capture ratios lead to increased yields and profits. Contributing to AND using 100% confidential, low or no cost reporting services like Smith Travel Research provide those meaningful numbers.

• **Technology** – These are times of declining labor pools, a thinning of middle management and growing customer demands for faster and better everything. Use technology as a performance enhancer, not as another assignment for the sake of a new report. There must be balance between "high tech" and "high touch." There are many training, purchasing, communication and improved customer satisfaction measurement tools tied to the Internet and technology.

• **Recognize that using the brand's reservation system as it is intended is usually a profit maker for your hotel.** Most central reservation referrals provide a rate far higher than what may have been quoted locally. Yes, there is a cost for distribution, but this a real value with the higher revenues from a guest who may have been concerned about things other than rate alone.

The bottom line to improving profitability rests with individual attention to your hotel's strengths AND weaknesses. Significantly improved service and guest relations come from being able to profitably operating your business.

.

◆　◆　◆　◆　◆

What are you selling?
In the factory we make cosmetics,
but in my stores we sell hope.

-Charles Revson, founder Revlon Cosmetics

◆　◆　◆　◆　◆

Chapter 31

It Should Take Two to Say NO

How do you decide if a piece of group business is a good or poor financial decision for the hotel? Is it better or worse to have the "bird in hand", a discounted piece of business or to wait, in yield management terms, for what could (but is not guaranteed to) be better?

In the mid-1980s, downtown Nashville was a very tough marketplace. While the city numbers were reasonably strong, but most of the group and higher rated markets were near the airport or the beautiful Opryland Hotel, Grand Old Opry and Opryland USA. The 300 rooms Sheraton Nashville would best be described as a "pleasant, business class, middle-aged hotel." It had two restaurants, a very quiet lounge and meeting space that could handle several hundred.

This hotel had a change of owners and sales team. The new team, comprised of an assortment of sophisticated to "down-home" sales styles, decided to embrace a balance of yield management with survivor tactics. They had a goal of X rooms for groups for each day of the year that was based on history, foreseeable changes in the marketplace and advanced bookings. They did not have the authority on their own to exceed the group targets, but they had both team and individual bonus potentials IF the rules were followed.

It wasn't easy and it took several months for them to figure out a system that worked. The team of David Livingston, Charlotte Martin, Alton Kelly, Charlotte Scheffer and J.R.

Davis discovered that requiring a second opinion on all potential bookings was not the administrative chore they feared. They found this second opinion usually lent an insight that was more profitable for the hotel and met the needs of the clients, while usually qualifying for their bonus potential.

The second opinion was invaluable because it regularly reminded the team of options, which could be considering other dates, creative meeting room set-ups or packaging with other companies. Sheraton Hotels with Worldwide Awards of Excellence in both Marketing and Public Relations acknowledged their efforts for their innovative approaches in very challenging economic times. Each of these sales professionals continued their careers in sales, with each rising to the director (or higher) level with different chains and management groups.

Chapter 32

Act As If You Are Number Two

If you were to poll a sampling of both the general public and frequent travelers to ask them who they thought was the largest car rental company, the answer would likely be the same in 2001 as it was in 1966: Hertz. The question was not which was the best, but the perceived largest. Identifying the "best" is too subjective a question and is very hard to qualify, as many companies rent the same brands of auto from similar locations.

Back in the late 1960s, Robert Townsend was an aggressive, open-minded, marketing focused CEO of one of Hertz' competitors. Try what he liked, he could not dent the market leadership of Hertz and was little more than a blip on the radar in some markets of other rental competitors.

Townsend and his team made an impact on the car rental business and on everyone else that has ever tried to overtake #1. The non-traditional way they accomplished their goal of significantly improving market share by "stealing" customers one at a time.

How did they do it? Their advertising slogan said it all: " We're only #2, so we try harder". Was Avis really #2 at that time? We'll probably never know, because the vital statistics (locations, number of rental units rented versus available, revenue generated, etc.) may not have been as detailed as they are today. What made Avis so well known was the way they became the underdog – everyone's favorite to succeed, especially against all those "other" brands.

Avis claimed the role of #2 by their own admission, but they "fought" with both Hertz and all the others to reach and maintain that coveted 2nd spot. Number Ones get to be and stay on top because they are regularly improving their service and product offerings.

Being part of the #1 brand might give your hotel a head start, but it remains up to the hotel sales staff to continue to prospect, research and book customers as if they are as hungry as Avis was back in 1970. It remains the responsibility of the operations staff to keep the hotel looking fresh, crisp, welcoming and attentive to the details.

Let the guests' letters and increased profits tell you of your successes. Let your heart tell you that you need to always retain the competitive spirit found in #2.

Common Sense Thoughts
on
Communication

◆ ◆ ◆ ◆ ◆

"Participation in community activities, done whole-heartedly, builds a free outside sales staff sending business to you."

—Don Campbell, former President, Hospitality
Motor Inns

(quote found in Educational Institute's Hospitality
for Sale)

◆ ◆ ◆ ◆ ◆

Chapter 33

Enthusiastic Attitude Will Pay Off For Hotel Salespeople

Having an enthusiastic attitude is important in being successful in any line of work. While there's nothing new about that maxim, it certainly bears repeating especially when you're talking about sales.

A lack of enthusiasm reflects a poor attitude. If a hotel salesperson or any staff members are not enthusiastic about his company, the hotel and its management and staff, and if he's not excited about meeting the needs of his customers, then there's a good chance he won't make the sale.

This is a critical consideration for an owner or owner/operator who does not feel comfortable or who does not like making sales calls. The general manager or owner is frequently the most effective person making sales calls due to the power of the title, but only if that person has enthusiasm.

Enthusiasm is the first observable aspect of a person's attitude, and a person can reflect it without ever having to speak a word. One's attitude is expressed mainly through non-verbal communication.

If you want proof of this, watch the people around you. Notice their facial expressions, their eyes, their body language, and their posture. Can you detect positive attitudes? Sure you can, it's easy.

Can people detect this in you? Of course.

Prospects will remember your enthusiasm or your deadpan message. Generally, we all like to associate socially and do business with people who have a positive attitude. While a prospect may not buy every time, he certainly will remember enthusiastic people the next time he's ready to book space for a client.

Of course, it's naive to think that every day is going to be a great day. With that in mind, can someone have a positive attitude even when he's having a bad day?

Certainly, successful professionals in all fields and consistent salespeople do it all the time. It requires a little acting sometimes, but it's mostly just a matter of putting a smile on your face.

There's something magic about a smile. First of all, it brightens one's own spirits. If you're having a bad day, feeling down, having the blahs or just tired, try this: Put on an act for an hour and smile. Have a "smile" in your voice when you're on the phone. Never walk by a person without saying "hello" with a smile. If you have a chance, look at yourself in the mirror with a smile — you'll notice the difference in yourself with an improved outlook.

We are not being overly optimistic here. It should only take an hour or so before you start feeling better about yourself and better about things in general. And you'll probably keep smiling and feel enthusiastic the rest of the day. Your associates may wonder what happened, but let them! That's their problem.

There's something about a smile that's contagious; like enthusiasm, a smile is catching. Another thing that is both self-motivating and contagious is whistling. It can't be something blue, but whistling a "happy" tune you like will positively turn heads, initiate conversations and make others smile.

It's great to work with people who are enthusiastic. As a salesperson for your hotel, you should be recognized as the most enthusiastic member of your property's staff. You will automatically be the "carrier" of this contagious thing that we call enthusiasm. Pretty soon the entire staff will get caught up in this wonderful feeling, and then what happens? The contagion starts spreading to the guests, and they start feeling good about staying at your property.

When you're out on calls, whether prospecting or selling, the proper attitudes will open doors. People who aren't enthusiastic don't make sales!

If a salesperson is enthusiastic about the property, it reflects confidence and seller's confidence results in buyer's confidence and again, it's catching.

There's no question about it: your attitude can help you sell more. Salespeople need to develop a special kind of attitude that makes them feel they will be successful. The ingredients for this special kind of "success attitude" include:

• A smile

• Enthusiasm for the company, including the property auditors, management, staff, service and quality

• A personal concern for the needs of your prospective customers.

This kind of attitude will also help lead to success within your own organization. All you need to do is follow this advice: "Be proud of where you work, so that where you work will be proud of you."

◆ ◆ ◆ ◆ ◆

Think of the world without salespeople. The following was taken from John Hancock Mutual Life (forerunner of the existing insurance giant): The sales person sells cars, tractors, radios, televisions, iceboxes and movies, health and leisure, ambition and fulfillment. The salesperson is America's emissary of abundance, Mr. And Mrs. High-Standard-of-Living in person. They ring the billion doorbells and enrich a billion lives. Without them, there'd be no American ships at sea, no busy factories and millions of fewer jobs. For the great American salesperson is the great civilizer and everywhere they go they leave people better off.

◆ ◆ ◆ ◆ ◆

Chapter 34

There Should Be No Such Thing As "Limited Service"

In the 2001 version of guides published by the American Automobile Association, there are a number of classifications for lodging types. By AAA definition, they include general descriptions of differing levels of food/beverage outlets, shops, conference/meeting facilities, ranges of recreation, entertainment options. The descriptions give an overview of size of the properties and an overview of common characteristics.

In general their range of classifications include:

- **Full Service**, with resorts and hotels in this category.

- **Limited Service** include condominiums, motor inns, apartments, cottage, motels and bed and breakfasts

- **Moderate Service** listings include ranches, country inns and lodges.

- **Further sub-classifications** include: suite, extended stay, historic and classic properties.

We are certainly not trying to challenge AAA overviews, as their intent is to provide meaningful interpretations of so many kinds of options. Their guides further point out the basis of their various diamond ratings. AAA has done a commendable job trying to explain the differences to the consumer and they do so substantially in product differentiation.

A major problem comes though, in our opinion , in the phrase "limited service" versus "full service". Full service usually implies those hotels with restaurants, lounges, meeting rooms and other product amenities.

The phrase "lodge" or "bed and breakfast" implies by name alone certain things to certain travelers, yet obviously these phrases alone do not mean enough. For example, by AAA definitions, bed and breakfast establishments are "usually smaller, owner operated establishment emphasizing an "away-from-home feeling". A continental or full, hot breakfast is included.

Many ROOMS ONLY establishments also serve breakfast and many have at least smaller meeting space, ranging from suites to meeting areas, breakfast rooms, etc. They have van drivers who act as bellmen. They have management team members who are outstanding hosts and hoteliers.

Former AH&LA Small Business Specialist Jerrold Boyer used to become very frustrated with managers who embraced the term "limited service." He used to remind hoteliers at educational and advisory seminars that the hospitality industry is indeed the SERVICE industry. His word of caution was that bigger did not necessarily mean better, nor did smaller automatically mean lesser.

There are many smaller, rooms-only properties that offer exceptional personalized attentiveness to their guests. It is the responsibility of the managers, owners and sales staff of those facilities to "sell" their staff and guests of the quality and extent of their service. There are many guests who might prefer smaller properties and staffs who elect to leave food operations to others.

If this industry is to continue to provide exceptional experiences for its guests and meaningful careers for its' staff, it must be attentive to its commitment to hospitality and not just "renting rooms."

"Limited service" - let's leave that image for the self-serve gas stations.

.

◆　◆　◆　◆　◆

Selling is a relationship and you build relationships systemically, not with a shotgun approach.

◆　◆　◆　◆　◆

Chapter 35

Sales Income Often Depends On incoming Phone Calls

First impressions often start with the switchboard or front desk with a basic phone call or inquiry. Many smaller to medium size hotels do not have separate telephone departments, but basic courtesy and professional handling of calls can make the difference of whether your hotel will even have a chance to be considered for the meetings market.

Meeting planners are continuously amazed by the lack of professionalism displayed by hotel salespeople in the performance of their jobs. From the handling of an inquiry to the solicitation effort to the booking stage and follow-up, salespeople need to be better performers.

From the start, we tend to put people in a bad frame of mind when incoming calls are answered tersely, unpleasantly or if the answer is so long that it comes out jumbled. We have all heard this "greeting" slurred together in one non-stop sentence:

"GoodMorning,ThankyouforcallingtheGreenTreeInnandCon ferenceCenter,wherethegrassisalwaysgreener,thisisTodd,may Ihelpyou? Oneminute,whileIputtheothercalleronholdplease...."

Whew! And all in 4 seconds or less!

Conversely, of course, a pleasant, understandable voice is a welcome sound to a caller, and can make the caller feel welcome and at ease. Well-operated hotels sometimes are reflected in the promptness by which the phone is being answered ,as well as the attitude of the hotel being displayed through the manner in which the call is taken.

As a starter, people calling in may be turned "on" or "turned off" by how the phone is answered. When the caller is connected to the sales or manager's office, the same opportunity exists to either impress or displease the caller.

How many times does the general manager's or sales department phone ring before it is answered? Once, ideally, and not more than twice, hopefully. Then, what is the attitude displayed by the secretary or sales- person answering the phone? A positive, friendly, eager-to-help voice is often the key to a successful sale.

Questions Can Be A Turn-Off

If the caller has to answer too many questions before he or she gets to the person wanted, the call (and possibly a lead or a piece of business) may be lost forever. Too often a caller has to answer questions such as: "Who may I say is calling?" "ah, what is the name of your company?" or "What is the nature of your call?"

These can all be real turn-offs. If the call is for a particular person in the sales office, it should be taken immediately and without questions. Salespeople should take every call without screening. Sometimes it is much easier getting through to the president of a large corporation than to the sales manager.

Sales personnel also should examine the number of calls they do not get right away, and how others handle those calls. If salespeople are out on the street making sales calls, which is something the caller is able to understand. If the salesperson being called is busy with a prospect, such as showing the hotel or helping plan a conference, that, too, is understandable. However, when a prospect or client calls and the salesperson is "in a meetings with other hotel people", the meeting should be interrupted so the salesperson can take the call. In fact, a good policy for salespeople to follow would be to have all in-house staff meetings before 9 a.m. or after 4 p.m. All other time in between needs to be available for selling.

Another area regarding the telephone is the length of time it takes to return phone calls. Some calls naturally have priority over others. This can usually be recognized by the name of the caller, the company name or the messages left. Many calls are made and messages left by what may appear to be "bothersome" callers; however, one never knows. The one call never responded to, which may have appeared to be a magazine sales representative trying to sell magazine advertising, could very well have been that person trying to setup a sales meeting for the people from the magazine,

It's good to prioritize telephone messages, but at the same time good salespeople always manage to respond to phone messages within 24 hours. The sales personnel at a property need to look at themselves and the manner in which they answer the phone. Enthusiasm shows up very easily, as does the lack of it. Then, they need to look at the sales secretaries and other people in the department and how the hotel main phone line is answered.

Let's all be enthusiastic and sell! After all, it is OUR livelihood – all of us !

◆ ◆ ◆ ◆ ◆

Mark Twain claimed it took him two weeks to prepare an impromptu speech.

◆ ◆ ◆ ◆ ◆

Chapter 36

Listen Carefully

A ll of us in hotel sales should wonder how much business we lose due to improperly handled telephone inquiries. A good percentage of initial contact for rooms business, meetings and catering is done by telephone. Even though initial contact may have been initiated through a personal sales call or advertisement, prospects generally will call by phone to check on availability of space and dates.

All too often, the person who answers the phone in the sales office is not prepared to take inquiries or answer questions. In many cases, they are not trained to ask specific, pertinent questions or even to listen properly.

See if this scenario looks familiar:

Prospect:	"Hi. My name is Howard Feiertag with the XYZ Corporation, and I'd like to know if you can handle a meeting for me on May 25th for fifty people."
Sales Person:	"I'm sorry, I didn't get your name."
Prospect:	"That's Feiertag. Howard Feiertag."
Sales Person:	"OK. When did you say you wanted a meeting?"
Prospect:	"May 25th"

Sales Person: "Thanks. How many people was that for?"

You get the idea. It can go on and on this way, and usually does.

The answer, of course, is for everyone in the sales office (or the front desk if you are at a smaller property) to be trained to listen carefully, ask the right questions, be knowledgeable and exude confidence. The prospect calling in must get the feeling that the person at the other end of the phone is a professional.

By using a worksheet appropriate to your hotel that covers all the questions that need to be answered, the person answering the inquiry will not only get all the questions answered, but will also sound professional. Avoid using writing tablets and pads of blank paper : —use only worksheets. Develop a personalized worksheet form with questions on it that cover all situations. This way, almost anyone can get the information on an inquiry.

An effective worksheet will include:

1. Prospect's name, title, company, address and phone number;

2. Name of the group for which the inquiry is being made;

3. Dates of meeting or function, number of sleeping rooms needed and number of nights of stay;

4. The reason for the request – an association committee meeting, a corporate sales meeting, a religious retreat, etc. This helps the hotel decide on the best way to meet the needs of the caller by helping the caller meet their needs. Different clients have different needs.

If your hotel has large meeting/banquet space, additional information may be helpful, including:

• Number of people attending and their breakdown (men, women, age groups, spouses, children);

• Daily schedule of activities;

• Group functions needed (breakfast, lunch, dinner, coffee breaks, receptions, special dietary needs, etc.);

• Social activities that you can assist in planning;

• Types of setups needed for each meeting-, space needed for exhibits, entertainment or demonstrations;

• Budget available;

• Who will make decision on location of the meeting, and when they can come to visit the property.

Obviously, worksheets can be elaborate, but it can be simplified. Arrangements for a local luncheon meeting, for example, would not require all these questions. The idea is to listen carefully to determine the prospect's needs.

If answers to the prospect's questions are not readily available, then the prospect should be told that someone would return the call as soon as possible. The worksheet is then passed on to someone who can handle the sale. Before the call is returned, all the information should be gathered so the prospect doesn't have to answer all the questions yet another time. All available information about the prospect and the group should be recorded.

It is important not to interrupt when prospects are talking Very often the things they say and how they say them can provide good tips that may help close a sale. Never feel uncomfortable about asking questions, as the more information available, the easier it is to close a deal.

Listening properly is hard work. It is one of the most important skills in closing a sale, but seldom is emphasized in our industry. Listening, unlike talking, never can get you into hot water.

Salespeople need to regularly look for ways of developing new business for rooms and food & beverage. Opportunities abound for all types of business. Knowing what's going on in the marketplace, checking on the competition and exploring new profit sources are important keys to success in sales.

And remember: be enthusiastic about what you're selling!

Chapter 37

Letter Writing Hints

Letter writing has become a lost art to many people today. With instant access e-mail and inexpensive phone calls, too many people have forgotten how to communicate properly and effectively in writing. Letters do remain a powerful tool for today's sales professional and using the written document can make a real difference to many clients.

The key to successful letter and proposal writing is usually expressed in one sentiment: Keep it simple. The purpose of letters is to get the reader's attention, so write conversationally.

A poorly written letter will start with "let me introduce myself," which is probably of little interest to the reader. A well written letter will grab the reader's attention, will tell a message, will meet the needs of the reader and finally will call the reader to action.

While there will always be exceptions (such as international conventions and trade shows of 40,000 attendees), most of us deal with manageable numbers of attendees/guests at our hotels. We invite you to consider the following as guidelines:

1. Make all letters personalized

2. If you are sending mass mailings, see rule #1. Remember that even Publishers Clearing House manages to do better than "occupant". Avoid the "fill in the name" look.

3. Keep your letters simple, crisp and to the point.

4. Try to keep your message to one page.

5. Do not make the reader feel uncomfortable – keep your message simple.

6. Do not be afraid of "white space" on letters. Even margins are easier on the eyes.

7. Remember that you are trying to convince someone of the advantages to them of selecting your hotel over your competitors. You are not trying to impress them with your vocabulary.

8. Remember to open letters with a benefit to the potential customer, while the last paragraph should direct the reader to action. State the message without overkill.

9. Be very careful of the spelling of the recipient's name and correct title.

10. Personally sign each letter legibly, preferably in blue ink to distinguish the signature from the color of the normally black printed message.

Using an appropriate P.S. (post script) at the end of a letter can be very effective, providing it contains an important message, such as a deadline or value.

Chapter 38

Solving The Problem Of Finding and Employing Problem Solvers

Think about it: when a guest decides to stay at your lodging facility, he or she has a problem that needs solving.

Away from home, a traveler faces the dilemma of not having a place to sleep, eat, conduct a meeting or be entertained. How well a hotelier solves that problem determines whether he will get that guests business in the months and years ahead.

But in order to solve our customers* problems, we need to start with solving our own.

Staff selection is a major one, for seemingly everyone in this business. In many cases, we select and employ people as a matter of expediency: a vacancy exists, and we have an urgency to fill a hole. We think first of getting the position filled, and then, secondarily, of how well we filled it.

This happens when an owner is looking for a manager, as often as it happens when a manager is looking for a night auditor or waitress or salesperson. The use of a poor approach in recruiting, interviewing, selecting, training, supervising and generally developing a staff is one of the most common problems in the hospitality industry. Yet the way those duties are handled is directly reflected in the amount of repeat business a hotel or motel gets.

Guests will return if their problems are solved; their problems will be solved if we employ problem solvers.

To be a problem solver, an employee has to sniff out and understand a customer's needs. He or she has to draw out those needs with smiles, friendly greetings, a warm "How may I help you?," an honest "It's a pleasure to serve you," or a sincere "Anything else I can do for you?"

Creating that magic in your property begins even before the selection process, when the initial candidates are still being interviewed. A check with references and interviews with the applicants will show if they have the credentials; explaining that the position is actually one of a professional problem solver will show you, by the applicant's reaction, if he has the ability. But even if you hire a problem solver, the employee still has to be trained and retrained to keep his or her skills up to par.

Communication is the best method, especially in maintaining a positive attitude. Schedule periodic meetings with all staff members, not just department heads. Make sure they know the communication process is two-way: they are there to give information as well as take it.

Another way of continually upgrading a staffs problem-solving abilities is by setting an example. If the person at the top is smiling, that attitude is going to pass through the ranks. Most importantly, a manager must not show his staff how to be a problem creator. He can't act stuffy, or too self-important. She can't avoid guests, or appear harried or unhappy.

Contrast him with the general manager who comes to work happy, with a healthy, warm "Hello!" for everyone, who at times checks out guests himself, pours coffee in the dining room, or personally conducts the staff meetings, and you'll put your finger on the difference between a good manager and one who should be working in another business.

Chapter 39

Understanding Body Language

The certification reviews for most of the Educational Institute of the American Hotel & Lodging Association include a section on communication. This section includes the facts on how written communication is best suited for technical, factual or legal effectiveness, vocal communication is best for sales.

The reason is not hard to grasp – we hear the spoken word, but it is our body language or verbal communication that tell us almost instantly if we have made a connection.

For example, if we send a direct mail piece about our hotel in Kentucky to a reader that has never been to the Blue Grass state, they will likely pitch the flyer as they have no connection. If they take a phone call from someone they know slightly about the Lexington area, they might have a possible interest in the University but they may not like doing business by phone. On the other hand, if we get a face-to-face meeting and "see" by the person's responses what motivates the person about the city – the ball team, the library, the gardens, architecture, the business department, the caliber of graduates from a certain program or whatever, then the connection is made.

There are entire books written about body language, but we offer the following as starting points:

1. Avoid putting obstructions between you and the other person, such as a briefcase, a package or presentation piece.

Don't sit behind a desk, but keep the communication flow smooth.

2. Learn about people's private space, which varies by gender, age and race. Don't make others feel uncomfortable.

3. Use your hands to demonstrate your point if that is your style, but don't point AT the other person.

4. Watch for people's habits, as some may be nervous, but others can be using negotiating and stall tactics.

5. Recognize what agreement signs are, such as subtle nodding, slight smiles and the inclination to complete the business being discussed.

6. Recognize what disagreement signs are such as wandering eyes, frowns or folded arms

7. Learn to read signs of closure or acceptance, such as crossed legs or leaning inwards.

It is important to observe as many body language signs as possible as quickly as possible to determine the best course of action with each person.

Chapter 40

Lobby Lizard

To someone who has never heard the phrase that is the title of this chapter, it might sound like a cross between an escaped (and probably unauthorized) "guest" and someone who might enjoy a lobby bar too regularly.

It is neither. What is it then? A lobby lizard is someone from hotel management who recognizes that customers in all kinds of businesses, especially service, respond positively to proper handling of service problems and complaints.

Statistically, figures we have seen for years in a variety of publications (ranging from the American Hotel & Lodging Association seminars to US News and World Report stories) reflect the reason why customers stop patronizing a business:

- 1% die
- 3% move
- 5% find a new friend in the business
- 9% go to a new or different competitor
- 14% have product dissatisfaction
- 68 % experience an attitude of staff indifference from one or more employees

In other chapters, we have stressed management/owner-ship visibility and responsiveness. Those in your organization responsible for sales need to inform, advise and persuade potential customers to use your hotel the first time. It is frequently the rest of the staff that must deliver the service AND sometimes correct a problem.

That is where a "lobby lizard" program can be a sales and service lifesaver. An effective program will have someone from management physically in the lobby at morning coffee and check-out times, talking with guests and demonstrating that this hotel is not indifferent to the minor annoyances that may be the unconscious reason that guest decides to go elsewhere next trip. It can be the GM, manager on duty, front office manager, executive housekeeper or whoever is suited to both listen and respond to problems. Management staff in uniform, such as the chef or engineer, can have a very positive impact.

All hotels have some kind of feedback system, ranging from welcome calls to comment cards to guest service hot lines. Many times these systems identify and perhaps handle the blatant problems, like a malfunctioning TV, a leaking showerhead or the wrong type of bedding. It is the "little" problems like the wrong wattage light bulb; the hour the housekeeper starts cleaning rooms rather loudly or the "acceptable" (but less than enjoyable) dinner in the hotel restaurant last night.

If our goal is return guests, then key success factors may include being away from the front desk or on the guest's "side" of the desk. Handling complaints and providing specific responses as quickly as possible, even if it means calling the guest later that day after they have checked out can mean the difference on the guest's future decision to return or not.

Look at those customer statistics again and don't let the "big one" happen at your hotel!

Common Sense Thoughts
on
Perspective

◆ ◆ ◆ ◆ ◆

The General Manager is the #1 salesperson. He/she must take part in:

1.guidance and direction of the staff

2.personal involvement with guest and personnel

3.meeting clients in the hotel

4.calling on at least one potential client each day

—Bob Durbin, former Executive Vice President,
Sheraton Hotels

(quote found in Educational Institute's Hospitality for Sale)

Chapter 41

A Self-Evaluation Test for General Managers

It is common knowledge and an undisputed fact that general managers at almost any size hotel could take over the sales efforts for that hotel and have the occupancy and RevPAR near the capacity level within just a few weeks.

Well, "almost" common knowledge and probably disputable.

Having been in both operations and sales at different points in our careers, we appreciate the value and contributions of each.

Here is a chance for General Managers to examine the other perspective.

Take a chance and think about your responses:

1. List your hotel's top 10 accounts, by individual and company name

2. How many in-house guests did you personally talk with this past week? (more than the good morning type of greeting)

3. How many regular guests did you call on the phone last week to say "thank you for using our hotel's services and asking if there is anything we can do better?"

4. How many local community activities did you personally attend the past week as your hotel's official representative?

5. How many outside sales calls did you make with the sales manager last week? If you don't have a sales manager, how many calls did you make alone?

6. What did you do between 11:30 am and 12:30 PM last Wednesday?

7. When did you personally last review sales files and call reports?

8. When was the last sales department/team meeting? Were you there?

9. When was the last time you personally called on the phone a guest who returned a comment card? (positive or negative comments)

10. How many hours did sales staff spend last week in non-productive sales activities?

Some possible responses:

1. Every GM should know the top 10. Contacts that the GM has may be different than others on staff, but regular networking (at least once per month per client) pays HUGE dividends.

2. Every GM should visit with at least 5 registered guests weekly, at morning coffee, at checkout, the restaurant, the pool, etc. These guests are prime candidates for repeat business or positive word of mouth promotion for your hotel, at virtually no cost.

3. Again, five is a workable, meaningful number for phoning regular guests.

4. The GM is the CEO of your hotel. Every organization, be it the Chamber of Commerce or the Kiwanis, welcomes and values the CEO. Involved CEOs are often a hotel's best sales person.

5. With no sales staff, a GM must make 3-5 calls per day on average to maintain, not gain ground. With a sales team, 8-10 calls per week can make a difference.

6. If a full service hotel, an effective GM will use this busy time of day to tour the restaurants, visit the kitchen, and perhaps pour coffee in a banquet, which will shock and definitely please most meeting attendees. If a rooms-only hotel, the GM should be having at least 2 business lunches per week. That's what your competitors are doing.

7. This one is not an open and shut case, as there are so many variables. Regular review of sales files is an acceptable answer, but this should be at least weekly, with personal follow-up with the sales manager.

8. Sales meetings should be before 8:30 am or after 5 PM to avoid prime contact and selling time. Successful teams value GMs who attend, offer support and occasional input.

9. The very small percentage of guests who take the time to tell what went well or wrong need to be TREASURED as resources by GMs. These people are the heart of word-of-mouth promotion. Call as many as you can – it will be worth it!

10. You know the answer to this one has to be that we have sales staff selling, not going to the bank, to the post office or the bakery. If we are going to steal market share, we need to be selling, not making change.

◆ ◆ ◆ ◆ ◆

Good salespeople do not sell the product or service. They sell the benefit of having that product or service.

For example, Americans each year buy several million ¼ inch drills. Not one of them wanted a drill - what they wanted was a ¼ inch hole. To get the holes, they had to get the drills.

◆ ◆ ◆ ◆ ◆

Chapter 42

Matching Benefits to Features

Televisions, radio, print and Internet advertising is becoming more visible for many hotel brands due to national identity building campaigns. It occurs to us that while brand building may be important for the stockholders of the public companies who want to increase market share for their brand of the whole, it does not automatically translate into market share for a specific hotel.

You, the reader of this book, are likely to be the owner, manager or sales staff of a specific hotel. It is our goal to help you increase your market share, guest satisfaction and profitability of your hotel.

In sales, to do that means communicating effectively to the prospect a very simple message: "what's in it for them." Every day, we are bombarded with more than 2,000 commercial messages that talk about everyone from apples to zoos. We are told in these commercials (usually by an announcer who is almost SHOUTING) that if we don't buy this brand of car TODAY that we will NEVER AGAIN be able to do so. We hear of "deals of the century" in everything from shoes to shock absorbers.

Hotel sales is really much simpler. We basically provide hospitality services, including lodging in a comfortable setting, food and entertainment to the traveling public. The "what's in it for me" question can be answered rather simply, by converting the features of our hotel into perceived benefits by our guests.

For example, many hotel today offer hair dryers. To someone like Michael Jordan, that is not particularly important to his decision on where to stay. To a family traveling on a week's vacation with two teenaged daughters, it means having to pack less which is a guest benefit resulting from a hotel feature. A pool can be a benefit to almost anyone, but only if it is open, appealing and has hours of operation that match your customers' needs.

It requires only a slight shift in perspective for both front desk agents and salespeople to identify the feature to benefit value, once the specific needs of the prospective guest is understood..

Examples might include:

1. In room coffee makers – the benefit to any guest who drinks coffee or tea is that they can have a cup while dressing in the morning and start their day "away from home" in a more leisurely and familiar way. It is convenient and available at no additional cost.

2. The hotel spa might be an unknown to many guests, but translating that feature into a way to "unwind" at the end of the day becomes a personal benefit for those interested.

3. A complimentary continental breakfast is a value appreciated by both those on a budget (government per diem travelers or school groups that had to raise money for their trip), as well as any traveler who appreciates a quick breakfast that did not require them to have to leave their hotel earlier in order to get something to eat. It is convenient and available at no additional cost.

4. Pre-assigned rooms means little to the walk-in who arrives at 10 PM without a reservation, but it means everything

to a tour group, to a school sports team or the VIP Corporate group that does not like to wait in line.

5. Non-smoking rooms are sometimes a controversial topic and have perhaps lesser interest in tobacco growing regions. To a non-smoker, the ability to reserve a guaranteed non-smoking room is frequently a deal breaker. They will be much more likely to confirm a reservation where they know they will get what is clearly to them – the "what's in it for me?" benefit.

What is critical in explaining the value of a feature is understanding the needs of the prospect. The feature explanation then should fit into meeting that need.

◆ ◆ ◆ ◆ ◆

Zig Ziglar revealed in his best-selling book, <u>Zig Ziglar's Secret of Closing the Sale</u>, how to overcome the objection: "it costs too much." Ziglar's reply: "The price is high, Mr. Prospect, but when you add the benefits of quality, subtract the disappointments of cheapness, multiply the pleasure of buying something good and divide the cost over a period of time, the arithmetic comes out in your favor...If it costs you a hundred dollars, but does you a thousand dollars worth of good, then by any yardstick you've bought a bargain, haven't you?"

◆ ◆ ◆ ◆ ◆

Chapter 43

The Use of Incentives Can Boost Revenues in Off-Peak Periods

The term "Off-peak" is not a universally understood phrase. What does that mean to you? If you are in Florida, it may mean the period when children are in school (late August to Christmas, early January to May). Yet those same markets have very high demand periods during certain holidays, such as US Thanksgiving, Christmas, Spring breaks, graduations, etc. In central and southern Arizona, the demand is even more from October to March with the seasonal "snowbirds", while the Grand Canyon marketplace suffers badly with severe cold in November to February. In Vermont or Vancouver, the periods between ski and summer are the challenges,

Off-peak today can offer an unbelievable opportunity for partnering with other companies in filling their needs, while filling space when we need it. Disney does this in Florida regularly, by offering significant packages and discounts to state residents in their off-peak time. Floridians are given incentives to enjoy Disney when the crowds are the lightest – a situation where "everyone wins".

Balancing your off-peak periods means thinking in some non-traditional ways and perhaps considering some of your franchise company's or state/province's discounting programs. Discounts alone do not increase demand automatically. Effective selling means matching the features of your hotel with the benefits of those features that are desired by consumers.

Here is a sampling of potential "partners" for your off-peak demand periods:

1. Auto dealerships, regardless of brand, are mostly independent licensees or franchisees that are very competitive in market share. Potentials here could be to use some of your unused product (rooms) as incentives for either their customer base or for their sales/service staff.

2. Banks have used the glamour and "get-away" appeal of hotels to generate new accounts.

3 Condominiums/Real Estate companies use hotel services and weekend packages as staff incentives or as client giveaways.

4 Dairy companies and other home delivery services offer hotel packages to their sales staff for creating new territories/accounts.

5. Local Insurance companies/agencies have found that hospitality options (hotels, golf, gaming, etc.) are excellent short-term incentives for weekly or monthly attainment of goals for agents.

6. Network Marketing organizations, ranging from giants like AMWAY, Mary Kay, and Avon appeal to newcomers for motivating new contacts as well as established producers. This is a largely untapped market, with huge potential as it crosses ethnic, geographic, age, gender and social boundaries. Like any of the above examples, the incentive of an unexpected mini-vacation has great appeal for many people.

7. Radio, cable and local TV stations are always looking for creative ways to reward listeners/viewers via contests, promotions, etc.

8. Retail stores are always seeking innovative packages to create traffic. Since most retail profits come in December,

much of their year is up and down and they are frequently motivated to promote, barter and be creative. Offering discounted gift certificates can be boon for both the retailer and the hotel.

All of these examples require personal networking by a hotel sales contact with someone from the company that is looking to enhance the appeal of their product or service. The payoff for hotels is increased traffic, revenues for otherwise unused product and additional promotional activity for your hotel through your joint participation.

◆　◆　◆　◆　◆

"Before everything else, getting ready is the secret of success."

—Henry Ford

◆　◆　◆　◆　◆

Chapter 44

Understanding the Basics of Market Segments

It would be truly fantastic if all it took to successfully operate a hotel anywhere in the world meant than offering clean, comfortable rooms at a fair price. The truth is, it requires offering that value to the right customers at the right time.

As we recognized in one of the very first chapters of this book, not every hotel can effectively and profitably meet the needs of every kind of guest every day. Many hotels serve multiple markets with some regularity, but those hotels that successfully accomplish serving those multiple markets identify and track the needs of those clients.

The following pages identify a cross-section of those markets and offer some ways to effectively meet their needs. This list is not meant to be comprehensive, but to offer two or three possibilities for each of these ten potential markets. We would estimate that most hotels can effectively and profitably serve up to 15-20 different market segments.

Get your team together to brainstorm about those markets that can give your hotel a high yield of reservations and satisfied guests. Recognize that not every hotel can serve effectively and profitably every market. For example, downtown Chicago or New York City is not the market for a trucking contract as they have no logical parking space for large trucks, while small town USA or Canada will not have opera companies. Pick and choose the markets accessible and logical, but be open-minded.

Literally all guests have some needs in common and we have not listed them in each worksheet. Some of those common ground areas include:

1. A range of bed types, including king sized (or at least queen) beds

2. Food available on property, or at least within walking distance

3. A cordial and efficient staff

4. Clean accommodations, with amenities appropriate to the service level and rates charged

5. Non-smoking rooms available that can be reserved in advance

6. Toll free reservations

7. Locations that suit the travelers needs

8. Assurance that guaranteed rooms will be held

9. Reliable telephone services, without excessive charges for local, toll free or internet access

10. Efficient check-in and check-out.

The following section details a number of markets and how savvy hotel sales people identify and match the needs of those customers with the services offered by their hotels. Items included are:

- **Customer Market Segment Definitions**
- **Traveler profile of this market segment**
- **Customer reason for traveling**
- **Value to hotel of this market segment**
- **Length of stay of this market segment**
- **Customer needs of this market segment**
- **How to tie hotel features into this customer needs and desired benefits**
- **How to find these customers**
- **Key contacts to selling to and servicing these customers**
- **Sales tools to assist you in this market segment**

Customer Market Segment
   • AAA/CAA ; American Automobile Association/Canadian Automobile Association members

Traveler Profile
   • A true cross section of travelers (numbering an estimated 50 million) consisting of singles, couples, families, seniors traveling substantially on personal travel

Customer Reason for Traveling
   •vacationers, reunions, family events

Value to Hotel
   • year round business, including weekends, holidays

Length of Stay
   • usually one or two nights

Customer Needs
   • AAA/CAA rates, family accommodations, recreation

How to Tie Hotel Features into Customer Benefits
   • AAA/CAA approval & rates, comforts of home (iron & board, microwave, connecting rooms, two double beds, in-room coffee, etc.) , playground/pool

How to Find Them
   • AAA tour books, travel agencies

Key contacts

> • AAA travel agents

Sales tools

> •Packages, prompt payment of commissions, ads in AAA travel books

Customer Market Segment
- Airports

Traveler profile
- Airline crews, distressed passengers, corporate & leisure travelers who prefer airport locations

Customer Reason for Traveling
- layovers, training, canceled flights, overnight stays

Value to Hotel
- Crews – year round, 365 day/year business; Distressed passengers – filler, walk-ins; Overnight demand for regular travelers who prefer airport locations

Length of stay
- Overnight

Customer needs
- Crews – transportation to/from the airport, food service, reliable wake-up service; Distressed passengers – airport transportation, food service, vouchers accepted, complimentary toiletries; Regular travelers - comforts of home (iron & board, microwave, in-room coffee, etc.), efficient service, shuttle service to airport

How to Tie Hotel Features into Customer Benefits
- Shuttle service, accurate airline billing, comforts of home (iron & board, microwave, in-room coffee, etc.), accepting vouchers, savings in taxis, auto rentals

How to Find Them

- Airline national offices; other hotels in your brand

Key Contacts

- Local managers of flight operations; national brand sales offices

Sales Tools

- Direct billing, incentives for crew satisfaction, airport advertising

Customer Market Segment
 • Associations

Traveler Profile
 • Members of professional, civic, fraternal, trade or service organizations

Customer Reason for Traveling
 • Annual conventions, regional meetings, board or committee meetings, trade shows, banquets

Value to Hotel
 • Weekday and weekend potential, depending on organization. Most are group related, with varying demands. Multiple occupancy, with related income, such as food, meetings, socials, entertainment, etc.

Length of Stay
 • From one to 4 nights

Customer Needs
 • Business services, meeting and food & beverage service, separate registration area, reliable message service, VIP rooms

How to Tie Hotel Features into Customer Benefits
 • Negotiable rates, flexibility, efficient services, pre-assigned rooms, voice mail, service oriented staff, meeting space

How to Find Them

• American Society of Association Executives, state or provincial chapter of association executives, leads from other hotels in brand, brand national sales office, Chamber of Commerce, Convention and Visitors' Bureau (CVB)

Key Contacts

• Executive Directors, Association officers or members, event planners

Sales Tools

• Ads in association publications, allied membership in association organizations, direct mail, active participation in CVB

Customer Market Segment

• Attractions, amusements

Traveler Profile

• Primarily leisure travelers & families; limited housing for performers

Customer Reason for Traveling

• Visiting theme parks, local or historical attractions, attending concerts or special performances

Value to Hotel

• Usually seasonal, with focus on summer, holiday and weekends. Multiple occupancy.

Length of Stay

• Usually one to three nights

Customer Needs

• Convenient location to site, discounted or packaged rates that include admission, family accommodations, pool/playground, children activities

How to Tie Hotel Features into Customer Benefits

• Package admissions or sell tickets at hotel; family rates, two bedded rooms, comforts of home (iron & board, microwave, in-room coffee, etc.), playground/recreation facilities

How to Find Them

• Local visitors guides, directories; Chamber of Commerce, Convention and Visitors' Bureau (CVB)

Key Contacts

• Business offices, park management, CVB leads

Sales Tools

•.Packages, active participation in CVB, targeted brochures highlighting hotel benefits to travelers, direct mail, local visitors guides

Lessons From the Field

Customer Market Segment

    Car rental agencies (rental customers)

Traveler Profile

- business travelers, vacationers, visitors to attractions

Customer reason for traveling:

- business and leisure travelers

Value to Hotel

- steady source of referrals, both weekday and weekend

Length of Stay:

- usually one to three nights

Customer Needs

- tie in with promotions, including frequent flyer credits; comforts of home (iron & board, microwave, in-room coffee, etc.) , playground/pool; convenient location to highways, attractions, etc.

How to Tie Hotel Features into Customer Benefits

- Partnership promotions with airlines, auto rental companies on site; essential services, food available, comforts of home (iron & board, microwave, in-room coffee, etc.) , playground/pool, free parking

How to find them

• Brand national sales office, Yellow Pages, visitor publications

Key contacts

• Car rental agency managers in your area

Sales tools:

• Partnership promotions, incentives or commissions for· referrals, brochures, personalized rack cards cross-promoting auto rental agency

Customer Market Segment

   • Referrals from Chamber of Commerce; Convention and Visitors' Bureau (CVB)

Traveler profile

   • Conventions and meetings of all sizes, openings of new business, malls, retail, new industry, city-wide events, etc.

Customer reason for traveling

   • Attendees to conventions; referrals of new businesses moving to area

Value to hotel

   • Source of new prospects

Length of stay

   • varies immensely

Customer needs

   • Varies by target market

How to tie hotel features into customer benefits

   • Varies by target market

How to find them

   • Membership in organization

Key contacts
- President, executive VP or director

Sales tools
- Varies by target market

It is important to remember that CVBs exist for both its' membership and the city, with their goal is to bring in as many visitors as possible. Your active support to them will usually be rewarded. Chambers of Commerce usually assume the duties of a CVB in smaller communities. As they have smaller staffs, they are not always able to respond to inquiries as quickly. Hotel support is critical to the hotel and the community.

Customer Market Segment

• Colleges/Universities/Schools

Traveler profile

• Wide range of travelers, including administrators, faculty, coaches, sports teams, academic event groups (debate/drama/chorales/dance), bands, alumni, parents and more

Customer reason for traveling

• Varies with market as above, including conferences, sporting events, performances, competitions, banquets, parades, reunions, graduations

Value to hotel

• Heavy weekend demand for some markets (especially group); Steady year round demand, depending on institution

Length of stay

• Varies – usually one to three nights

Customer needs

• Competitive rates, meeting places, flexibility with arrival/departure, complimentary breakfast, bus parking, location near where they need to be

How to tie hotel features into customer benefits

• Staff open to last minute changes, baggage handling, food service, pre-registration, additional security, and hospitality rooms. Welcome reception

How to find them

• Brand national sales office; other hotels in brand; campus directories

Key contacts

•.Varies immensely, but includes: admissions, business office, purchasing, President's office, Dean of Students, athletic directors, individual department or club chair, student activities, coaches

Sales tools

• Direct mail; personal contacts/calls/visits, brochures, groups rates, barter of ad for hotel services throughout the year

Certain high schools and community colleges can have as much demand for many hotels as higher profile four-year universities.

Customer Market Segment
- Corporations and companies

Traveler Profile
- Individuals and groups traveling on business

Customer Reason for Traveling
- Business travel , training programs, interviews, seminars, branch openings, banquets, etc.

Value to Hotel
- Week-day demand for roughly 46 weeks per year.

Length of Stay
- Varies, usually one to three nights

Customer Needs
- Negotiated rate, business services, food available, meeting facilities at least nearby, reliable message & wake-up services, King beds, cable, exercise room, data port, free in room coffee

How to Tie Hotel Features into Customer Benefits
- Corporate rates, pre-assigned rooms, efficient service, reliable telephone services without excessive charges for local, toll free or internet access, accurate billing, food and meeting space, free newspaper, free airport transportation (if applicable)

How to Find Them

   • Chamber of Commerce, Local business directories, Internet, Yellow Pages, business section of newspapers, local chapters of Meeting Planners International and Society of Corporate Meeting Planners, leads from in house guests

Key Contacts

   • Department heads, travel agents and planners, training directors, sales managers, communications departments, secretaries, corporate travel managers

Sales Tools

   • Direct bill capabilities; tie in with promotions, including frequent flyer credits; brochures, personal contacts/calls/visits

Customer Market Segment
- Government Agencies

Traveler profile
- Individuals and groups traveling on local, city, state/province, county and federal government business. Sequestered juries.

Customer reason for traveling
- training programs, interviews, seminars, recruiting programs, audits, meetings, banquets, hearings, trials

Value to hotel
- Government rates, which can range dramatically from local to federal; generally week-day demand for roughly 46 weeks per year.

Length of stay
- Varies, usually one to three nights, except for juries, which is of indeterminate length.

Customer needs
- Guaranteed per diem rate, business services, food available, meeting facilities, reliable message & wake-up services, data ports

How to tie hotel features into customer benefits
- Tax exemption rates in some cases ; pre-assigned rooms, efficient service, reliable telephone services without

excessive charges for local, toll free or internet access, accurate billing, food and meeting space

How to find them

• Chamber of Commerce, Local business directories, Internet, Government section of Yellow Pages, local newspapers, Society of Government Meeting Planners directory, Society of Government Travel Planners, leads from in house guests, brand national sales offices, SATO offices

Key contacts

• Department heads, travel planners, training directors, secretaries, Sheriff's office (for juries), government recruiting offices, Government Service Administration (GSA) offices

Sales tools

• Direct bill capabilities; tie in with promotions, including frequent flyer credits, brochures, personal contacts/calls/visits

Customer Market Segment
  · Religious

Traveler profile
  · Individuals, families, groups, guest speakers, clergy, youth groups

Customer reason for traveling
  · special services, seminars, retreats, camps, religious study, training, performances, marriage or singles encounters, funerals, weddings, baptisms, reunions

Value to hotel
  ·.Steady source of repeat year round business and referrals. Heavy weekend demand, multiple occupancy.

Length of stay
  · Varies – usually one or two nights

Customer needs
  ·.Family accommodations, convenient location, connecting rooms, tax exemptions for certain programs, negotiated rates, and community involvement.

How to tie hotel features into customer benefits
  · No adult movies, rate flexibility, barter or contribute rooms for distressed referrals from church

How to find them

• Chamber of Commerce, Yellow Pages, local newspaper, leads from in house guests and staff, local churches, Religious Conference Managers Association (RCMA)

Key contact

• Minister, rabbi, priest; church secretary, business manager, choir director, youth director, study group leader.

Sales tools

• Ad in church publication, brochures highlighting hotel services to church needs, direct mail, newsletter, trade outs, direct billing

◆　◆　◆　◆　◆

Good fortune is what happens when opportunity meets with preparation."

-Thomas Edison

◆　◆　◆　◆　◆

Common Sense Thoughts on the Inner Workings of a Successful Hotel Sales Effort

The most productive sales instruments are personal selling and phone selling. There are no other sales instruments. All the rest make other people rich. Personal selling and telephone selling are measurable, reliable and most effective.

Industry leader Michael Leven, quoted while serving as Senior Vice President of Marketing, Americana Hotels

(quote found in Educational Institute's Hospitality for Sale)

Chapter 45

Using the Sales Staff Effectively
Or
The Sales Staff Must Have Time to Sell

"**I**t" happens everywhere, regardless of the brand, the location or the type of hotel. "It" happens more at medium and smaller sized hotels (under 200 rooms), but we have seen "it" at 600 room convention hotels.

The "it", of course, is the extent to which on non-sales jobs to which sales staff are frequently assigned. The problem comes when the sales manager or team is regularly expected to:

1. Work the front desk all day

2. Work the restaurant as a cashier or greeter

3. Answer the hotel switchboard

4. Set up meeting rooms

5. Go to the bank, the post office, the printer

6. Stuff envelopes for accounting

7. Post the daily function board

8. Run the entire 3 day client meeting

9. and the list goes on.........................

There is a natural "tug" between operations and sales staff. Operational staff see sales people lunching with clients and imagine extravagant expense account trips. The truths lie in between those imagined extravagances and the "grunt" work of converting leads and prospects into confirmed business. There is a TEAM effort in successful hotels where on occasion the sales manager may do the above tasks or pour coffee in the restaurant, but to the ongoing detriment of selling.

Effective managers will want to make sure their sales team is out selling during every logical time. Using the sales staff regularly for the above listed jobs might save a few dollars today on payroll or make it slightly easier for others on the staff. Without question, though, it will cost your hotel substantially more tomorrow with no new business because your competition "stole" it by having their sales people there making the personal contacts.

Continual identification and development of new and repeat business cannot be completed by a cashier or front desk agent, but only by a trained and competent professional versed in the hotel's offerings, pricing and selling tactics.

The value of the person responsible for selling is a matter of financial prioritizing and strategic planning. Larger hotels find the challenge a bit easier sometimes as they have more support staff. Owners and managers of every size of hotels must realize that someone must be developing new prospects for the future, because competition, the economy and other market changes will erode some of the existing base of business.

In smaller hotels where the general manager might be the sales staff as well, there needs to be additional staff trained to do the every day business chores so the GM can effectively be out in the marketplace, finding the business to keep everyone gainfully employed.

Chapter 46

The Importance of Job Descriptions

Job descriptions aid in the hiring process by defining the specific criteria needed to effectively fill a position. Not only do they assure the proper criteria are being considered, but they aid in keeping all interviews as objective as possible. They provide the necessary criteria on which to structure the interview itself and assure all applicants of being evaluated fairly and equally. They may also provide legal protection to the property and interviewer alike by defining the specific skills required by an applicant to qualify for the job.

It is the responsibility of the general manager and sales director to develop job descriptions for every position in the sales office.

Today, regardless of the size of a property, many sales department heads have the title of "Director of Sales." This can help position your sales representative as an equal when competing with other hotels. It is prudent to be certain that your sales staff is trained well enough to be able to compete, as a title alone does not make up for inadequately prepared person. Additional sales personnel (except clerical) may use the title of Sales Manager. This gives greater dignity to both positions and makes each more effective in dealing with their clients. A job description also clarifies the functions of each position.

The size of the Sales Department is dependent on the size of the hotel; however, at the least, the Director of Sales should be given whatever some administrative assistance if at all possible to maintain an effective program, such as correspondence, computer or function book entries, answering the telephone, messages, filing, etc. This assures that the sales representative is spending the majority of time "selling" and bringing in revenue to the property. A properly written job description for a sales administrative assistant would define these functions.

The following pages provide sample job descriptions for a Director of Sales and a Sales Manager (or Sales Representative). Please remember that your may vary in needs and specific duties and that these are offered as starting points and suggestions only. We have found that there are many properties that have titles that do not actually tie into the functions or duties of the person. We urge prudence and caution in titles – make them meaningful!

Position Description

Title: Director of Sales and Marketing

Reports to: General Manager

Position Summary

• Identifies, develops, and maintains property sales and marketing objectives, plans, and programs in accordance with the hotel's mission statement.

• Oversees the Sales Managers, Catering Managers and support staff as appropriate.

Tasks and Competencies

1. Assists hotel management by acting as "first contact" with all outside creative talent (i.e., photographers, graphic artists, printers) to insure that the target market and image positioning is clearly communicated to all involved in the creation of collateral sales materials and advertising campaign strategies.

2. Maintains high visibility in the surrounding community and in the hospitality community as appropriate within the brand or ownership group.

3. Maintains efficient sales office procedures for productive use of staff time and insures the maintenance of accurate and updated account files and follow-up procedures.

4. Monitors and directs sales leads to outside sales managers, provides motivation, support, encouragement, and direc-

tion to all members of the sales department. Makes face-to-face sales calls.

5. Assists in the creation of the Marketing and Sales plans.

6. Maintains all sales systems, such as sales records and reports, conference calendar, traces of history and potentials, logs of groups not previously accommodated and mailing lists.

7. Develops design of new programs and campaigns, designed to develop additional sales from the various market segments.

8. Ensures the prompt and systematic servicing of all business accounts (i.e., tracing, booking, contracting, communicating with hotel departments, and following up with group for feedback and future bookings).

9. Identifies and analyzes competition, both locally and regionally.

10. Works with brand and management company team to insure optimum results in cooperative sales, marketing and advertisement campaigns

Pre-Requisites:
• **.Education:** College degree in business management, hotel management, or marketing preferable. Successful hospitality or sales careers can enhance this.

- **Communication:** Must be able to speak, read, write, and understand the primary language(s) used in the workplace and by guests who frequently visit the workplace.

- **Experience:** Previous hotel-related experience, sales management experience in hotel or service industry, experience in budgeting and business planning.

- **Physical:** Requires manual dexterity, grasping, writing, standing, sitting, walking, repetitive motions, visual acuity, hearing, writing, and excellent speaking ability.

- **Technological:** Must be competent in computer skills (word processing, spreadsheets, data base). Background in automated sales office systems is helpful.

Position Description

Title: Sales Manager

Reports to: Director of Sales or General Manager

Position Summary

 • Identifies, develops and maintains property sales objectives, sales plans, and programs in accordance with the hotel's mission statement.

 • Outside sales calls are a priority in this position. Must have a vehicle to use for outside sales calls that is in good condition, insured, and the person must have a current driver's license.

Tasks and Competencies

 1. Maintains high visibility in the surrounding community and in the hospitality community as appropriate.

 2. Maintains efficient sales office procedures and insures the maintenance of accurate and updated account files and follow-up procedures.

 3. Directs sales leads to outside sales reps, provides motivation, support, encouragement, and direction to all members of the sales department. Makes face-to- face sales calls.

 4. Maintains all sales systems, such as sales records and reports, conference calendar, traces of history and potentials, logs of groups not previously accommodated and mailing lists.

5. Designs new programs and sales campaigns, to develop additional sales from the various market niches.

6. Ensures the prompt and systematic servicing of all business accounts (i.e., tracing, booking, contracting, communicating with hotel departments, and following up with group for feedback and future bookings).

7. Identifies and analyzes competition, both locally and regionally.

8. Follows the Sales and Marketing plans

Pre-Requisites

• **Education:** College degree in business management, hotel management, or marketing preferable. Successful hospitality or sales careers can enhance this.

• **Communication:** Must be able to speak, read, write, and understand the primary language(s) used in the workplace and by guests who frequently visit the workplace.

• **Experience:** Previous hotel-related experience, sales management experience in hotel or service industry, experience in budgeting and business planning.

• **Physical:** Requires manual dexterity, grasping, writing, standing, sitting, walking, repetitive motions, visual acuity, hearing, writing, and excellent speaking ability.

• **Technological**: Must be competent in computer skills (word processing, spreadsheets, data base). Background in automated sales office systems is helpful.

Chapter 47

Possible Sources and Methods of Recruiting Qualified Individuals

When a determination has been made that there is a need and a position to be filled and a realistic job description complete, the next step is to recruit applicants.

The following is a list of possible sources and methods.
- Promotion from within
- Word of mouth via staff
- Trade schools
- Business Colleges
- Community or Junior Colleges
- Universities
- Night or continuing education schools
- Church bulletins
- Resources-vendors-sales people
- Customers referred by present employees
- Fraternal organizations (Moose, Elk, etc.)
- Business groups (Rotary, Kiwanis, etc.)
- .Professional associations (Hotel Sales Management Association)

- National Association for Professional Sales Women, and Sales and Marketing Executives
- Social groups, Welcome Wagon, etc.
- Chamber of Commerce referral
- Retired Military
- Recent relocations to your area (realtors)
- Classified advertising
- Display advertising
- Career days in schools
- Other properties in town
- Other properties in brand or in management company
- Trade publications
- Search firms
- State employment agencies
- Temporary help agencies

Chapter 48

Factors for Successful Interviewing

1. Plan your interview. Thoroughly review the job descriptions and specific job requirements. Decide which skills are most critical and important.

2. Create your interview plan. Formulate job related questions that will help the interviewee give behavioral examples. Do not use hypothetical questions that should show how a person handled specific tasks or situations in the past. Write out your questions.

3. Arrange for an interview environment. Make sure there are no interruptions. See that the interviewee is comfortable. Plan for enough time. An out of your office setting is best to help relax the interviewee and allows you to avoid interruptions.

4. Conduct the interview. Use rapport-building questions. Ask open-ended questions. Allow silence. Seek contrary evidence. Control the interview. Gain behavioral examples.

5. Use intuition to help you ask better questions. Confirm or refute your gut feeling. Protect other people from your hidden biases or prejudices.

Suggestions to Remember in the Interview Process:

- Rate skills.
- One behavioral example may provide evidence for or against several skills.
- No one is absolutely perfect or absolutely bad.
- Ask yourself if you have enough information to do a good rating.
- Allow for unmeasured skills.

Chapter 49

Sample Interview Questions

A wide variety of questions can be used to help gain information about a candidate's job skills. Use these questions as guides to help you develop questions that target a specific job's skill requirements.

General Questions

1. Describe a time on any job when you were faced with problems or stresses that tested your coping skills. What did you do?

2. Give an example of a time that you had to keep from speaking or not finishing a task because you did not have enough information to come to a good decision. Be specific.

3. Give an example of a time when you had to be relatively quick in coming to a decision.

4. Tell me about a time when you had to use your spoken communication skills in order to get a point across that was important to you.

5. Can you tell me about a job experience in which you had to speak up in order to be sure that other people knew what you thought or felt?

6. Give me an example of a time when you felt you were able to build motivation in your co-workers or subordinates at work.

7. Give me an example of a specific occasion in which you conformed to a policy in which you did not agree.

8. Describe a situation in which you felt it necessary to be very attentive and vigilant in your environment.

9. Give me an example of a time when you had to use your fact-finding skills to gain information for solving a problem. Then tell me how you analyzed the information to come to a decision.

10. Give me an example of an important goal that you set in the past and tell me about your success in reaching it.

11. Describe the most significant written document, report or presentation that you have had to complete.

Specific Questions You Might Ask About Sales, Catering or Convention Service backgrounds

Skills critical for success:

• Organizational--Can delegate and work through people.

• Supervisory--Can oversee the work of other people.

• Versatility--Willing and capable of being flexible.

• Interpersonal relations--Can get along with people.

• Communication with employees and guests--Possesses good oral and written communication skills.

• |Responsible--Dependable, follows through.

• Detail oriented--Does not take things for granted.

1. Give an example of when you handled a function that was off-schedule.

2. Tell me about a time when you had to organize an event that involved multiple departments and what you did to create a teamwork environment.

3. Describe a time when you had to handle a person or group of people under the influence of alcohol and out of control. How did you handle it?

4. Describe a time when a deal you put together seemed to fall apart. What action did you take to salvage the situation?

5. Recall a time when you had a very dissatisfied customer and what you did to appease the customer and get him/her to use your services again?

6. Give an example of when you were in direct competition with another hotel. What did you do to get the business?

7. What do you rate as success factors?

8. How do you pace your work load?

9. How do you meet deadlines?

10. How do your prioritize your work week?

◆ ◆ ◆ ◆ ◆

Networking is being able to help or benefit from individuals you directly have a relationship with to achieve life's ends.

-Paul Drolson, division manager, American Express

◆ ◆ ◆ ◆ ◆

Chapter 50

Office Space

Location & Appearance of a Sales Office

The sales office makes a valuable first impression on a potential client of your hotel. The location and appearance of this office make a statement about the property's selling philosophy. A sales office that is easy to find, tastefully appointed, free of clutter and comfortable tells the prospects that you and your hotel cares and wants their business.

"Do's" and "Don'ts" Relating to the Sales Office Space

Positive Things to Do

  • Have the office accessible to meeting and banquet facilities and easy to find from hotel lobby. Location adjacent to conference room for group meetings.·

  • Make the space private for guest comfort level and staff effectiveness.·

  • Display on the wall photographs of events, celebrities or other important local happenings hosted at the hotel, highlighting guest rooms, meeting rooms, service staff, and appropriate awards.·

• Have tasteful furniture in excellent repair. There should comfortable chairs for a reasonable number of visitors, ideally for 2-6 people.·

• Good ventilation, heat and air conditioning should be properly controlled from the office.·

• In larger hotels, a receptionist or secretary should be properly trained to offer and promptly serve refreshments. This person should also be trained to provide photographs and other information highlighting hotel banquets, creative breaks, menus, set-ups, and general hotel information, etc. In smaller hotels, the front desk agent or whoever directs guests to sales should be courteous, offer seating or refreshments as possible and remain attentive to waiting guests.·

• The reception and seating area should have current trade publications, regional items (travel, cook books, etc.), popular magazines and hotel information.·

• Fresh flowers or plants are always a positive.·

Clean windows and proper control of sunlight should not be overlooked.·

• A well-lighted room is conducive to both staff and visitors.·   A centerpiece (wine, floral, etc.) featured in a larger sales area can be a sales tool.·

• Lobby area can be used as a possible waiting or reception area, but it must be fresh and have as much of the above items as possible.·

• All front desk personnel must have training as to how to greet people looking to discuss possible bookings, and rehearsed script can fill that need.·

• All required information ready, such as brochures, menus, contracts, price lists, etc.) must be immediately accessible in the sales office.

Negative Things to Avoid

• Locating sales offices in out-of-way place such as basement or back guest room gives a poor impression of the hotel's regard for the sales effort.

• There must be some level of privacy for quoting rates and handling negotiations.

• The "Fishbowl", a glassed-in area within lobby, means the sales person is likely to be called for many non-sales activities.

• A freestanding desk in lobby has the same problem and means this will become information central.

• Files stacked on floor, distasteful pictures, calendars displayed near desk areas and general clutter give a poor impression of the hotel overall.

• Cardboard boxes, bags, stacking of magazines, etc. likewise do not give the potential customer a sense of order in what they may be buying.

• We all have to live within our budgets, but old, dated lobby furniture or any "worn" look in furnishings gives the potential customer a probable warning signal of the quality and "image" of the hotel. There are tasteful ways to affordably handle this.

• Not all hotels have a secretary or receptionist to deal with customers upon arrival, but an unprepared front desk agent can effectively "kill" a potential booking with an uncaring or disinterested attitude or with flippant remarks.

◆ ◆ ◆ ◆ ◆

Networking can increase profitability.Remember the holiday feel-good movie, Miracle on 34th Street, in which Macy's and Gimbels broke tradition by cooperating rather than competing? Both firms ended up having the greatest Christmas profits ever.

—Theodore Levitt, Harvard University

Closing Thoughts

◆　◆　◆　◆　◆

The most effective way to promote business is to rely on word-of-mouth promotion. This boils down to common sense, good value for money, and good service."

—Paddy Fitzpatrick, Owner, Fitzpatrick's Castle Hotel, Killiney, Ireland and Fitzpatrick's Shannon Shamrock, Bunratty, Ireland

(quote found in Educational Institute's Hospitality for Sale)

◆　◆　◆　◆　◆

The Single Most Effective Sales Tool There Has Ever Been

If you were to ask almost anyone the most effective means of reaching a potential client, there might be differing answers. Some people might say memorable advertising, while others say it is image or identity. Some people might offer that discounting is the best way to reach the most people, while others live and die by habits, computer formulas of adjusting rates or of great promotional gimmicks that get customers attention.

We are going to ask you to stop reading for just a moment and think of what is your personal favorite restaurant. Imagine it in your mind.

What do you recall about this restaurant? Is it the food? The location? The view? The prices? The service? Their advertising?

Or is it a combination of the above that makes this place stand out from the literally hundreds of food choices you have at your disposal within one hour of where you likely live?

The single most effective sales tool there has ever been is something that we all understand, yet find it hard to capture because it is so personal.

That something is called **"word of mouth"** and it is indeed the most successful and effective of any sales tool available. It works because it is special to the individual, yet it is something that most people want to share.

Positive "word of mouth" can remove the negatives of an awkward access to a hotel's front entrance or to the fact that your hotel is actually three blocks away from the beach. It can overcome rate sensitivity or that your hotel does not have a gourmet dining room.

Our opening thoughts in this book as a sharing of ideas reflected that the world of hospitality sales has changed over the years from what it may have once been. Realizing that much of what was always strong and positive about effective hotel sales today still includes the need for sincere and personal contact, a heartfelt hand-shake, a warm smile and a personal commitment. Creating a positive word of mouth experience at your hotel is part of a culture that has never been more important.

Appendix

There are many terms, abbreviations and slang words used in the hospitality industry that are not universally understood. As many people regularly join the industry from other fields, we have provided some additional terminology. and identified some of the more frequently used terms.

Some of those phrases are used mainly in sales. Others are primarily operational in nature. In larger, full service hotels, the Rooms Division will include those departments that service the non-food and beverage areas. The largest of those departments are Front Office and Housekeeping.

Hotels of all sizes and levels of service all have both a centralized office (the front desk area) and a center for cleaning the facility, the housekeeping department.

Industry Terms to Know

Accommodate

A promise of a room for a guest - if not in that property, then a commitment to find a room elsewhere.

Adjoining rooms

Two or more rooms side by side without a connecting door between them. In other words, rooms can be adjoining without being connected. Most families traveling with smaller or younger children prefer connecting rooms.

ADA

The US Congress enacted the American with Disabilities Act in the 1990s to accommodate the needs of both guests and staff. The law has specific guidelines about making reasonable accommodations in meeting the needs of both. Check with your hotel association, brand management or legal counsel with questions.

Adjust/Adjustment

A correction of an error that occurred on a previous day.

Advance Deposit

Pre-payment of room charges. A deposit the guest furnishes for a room reservation that the hotel is holding.

Advertising Agency

A company that furnishes advertising and marketing services to clients. Ad agencies may be paid by a commission from the media or a predetermined fee from the client.

(Advertising) Agency Commission

A commission the media pays to an advertising agency. It is expressed as a percentage (usually 15%) of the gross advertising rate.

(Advertising Agency Fee

A dollar amount agreed upon, in advance, by the agency and client, which compensates the agency for all services in lieu of commission.

Affiliated Hotel

One of a chain, franchise, or referral system. Membership features include special services, such as a national reservations system, a global or national identity through an advertising campaign, purchasing savings, financing options and other potential advantages which are paid for by fees or royalties to the organizing or franchise company.

A.H.

Airline crews have special travel schedules and needs sometimes need to have rooms "held over."

AH&LA

American Hotel and Lodging Association

AIDA

An acronym for attention, interest, desire, and action, which is a formula, designed to catch customers' attention, get them interested, create a desire to buy, and generate action.

Airport Hotel

A hotel located near a public airport. Airport hotels vary widely in size and service level.

A La Carte

A term that describes meal items priced separately on the menu.

All-Expense Tour

A tour offering all or most services – transportation, lodging, meals, sightseeing, and so on - for a pre-established price. The terms "all-expense" and "all-inclusive" are much misused, as virtually no tour rate covers everything. The terms and conditions of a tour contract should specify exactly what is covered.

Amenity

Item the hotel provides to make the guest feel more at home. Most are complimentary, but there may be a charge. Items such as

shampoo, irons & ironing boards, coffee in the room are all amenities.

American Bus Association

A trade association of U.S. motor coach operators with the mission with the purpose of promoting member professionalism and motor coach tour development. Many hotels and attractions belong as allied members to network, seek business and network with tour operators. Many hotels and attractions belong as allied members to network, seek business and network with tour operators.

American Hotel & Lodging Association

(the word "lodging replaced the word "motel" in 2001 to expand the many options now part of the industry) A federation of state and regional hotel membership associations, which offers benefits and services to hospitality properties and suppliers. AH&MA reviews proposed legislation affecting hotels, sponsors seminars and group study programs, conducts research, and publishes Lodging magazine. The Educational Institute of AH&MA is the world's largest developer of hospitality industry training materials, including textbooks, videotapes, seminars, courses, and software.

American Plan

A room rate that includes three meals. These are primarily used at resorts and conference center locations.

American Society of Travel Agents

A trade association of travel agents, tour operators, and suppliers to the industry with worldwide membership exceeding 13,000. Purpose is to promote and advance the interests of the travel agency industry and safeguard the traveling public against unethical practices.

AMTRAK

The name under which the National Railroad Passenger Corporation operates almost all U.S. inter-city passenger trains. The inter-city trains are usually operated under contract with individual railroads.

Arrival

Time of day of guest check-in:

1. Early - arrival early in day
2. Late - arrival late in day

Attraction

A natural or synthetic facility, location, or activity which offers items of specific interest, such as a natural or scenic wonder, a theme park, a cultural or historic exhibition, or a wildlife/ecological park.

Audience

A group of households or individuals who listen to, view, or read a communications medium.

Audience Profile

A description of the characteristics (sex, age, income, etc.) of individuals or households exposed to a medium. It may also refer to the minute-by-minute viewing pattern of a television, cable or radio program or advertisement.

Average Daily Rate(ADR)

The average of all rates charged for all occupied guest rooms during one day of business. The method of computing the ADR is to add the total of all guest room revenues and divide that by number of rooms sold.

Back of the House

The functional areas of a hotel in which personnel have little or no direct guest contact, such as the laundry, engineering and accounting. A more positive term to use to demonstrate staff appreciation might be "Heart of the Hotel."

Bank

Funds issued to cashier for handling guest transactions, which must be balanced at the beginning of each shift.

Banquet

A formal dinner for a group, usually in a private room with a pre-selected menu. Some banquets have entertainment or speeches following the meal.

Banquet Contract

The legal form used between hotel and client to confirm banquet arrangements, including guarantees, services agreed upon and payment terms.

Banquet Captain

A supervisor who directs the banquet crew, and oversees functions.

Billboard

A large panel designed to carry outdoor advertising along the highway. Options include painted or papered boards, as well as newer styles that have rotating messages. Costs for billboards vary tremendously depending on location of board, measurable traffic that view the message each day, the length of contract the advertiser agrees to and the overall market.

Block

A group of rooms held at the request of Sales or Catering to fulfill a commitment made to an organized group.

Booking Agreement Reference

material for a number of reservations made by a company or a group.

Book

To sell hotel space, either to an individual or to a group needing a block of rooms.

Breakout Meeting

A meeting that supplements a convention or larger meeting. They are always smaller, as they go to sub-topics of the main group.

Brochure

A printed folder containing descriptive or advertising material.

They range from simple stock cards promoting a special rate or program to four color, multi-fold variations with an advertising or descriptive message.

Bucket

A tray used for filing guest folios by room number at the Front Desk.

Bucket Check

A morning and afternoon comparison of guest bucket folios with the room rack or computer data base to verify the accuracy of accounts and that all rooms are in fact occupied by the guest whose information is at the desk. A manual comparison of all occupied rooms with the housekeepers' inspection report and the numerical listing of rooms in the bucket is done daily (late afternoon) to make sure of an accurate inventory of available rooms.

Budget

A detailed financial projection of all projected revenues and expenses for a hotel for a given period, usually one year. This includes all departments and both operating and long-term obligations.

Budget Hotels

Rooms-only properties that offer few amenities or services and are at the lower end of the price range of offerings. Also called economy hotels.

Buffet

An assortment of foods offered on a table in self-service fashion.

These can be offered either in a banquet or a restaurant setting and are usually offered at an all-inclusive price.

Bus

In the travel industry, the word "bus" is reserved for a vehicle that provides scheduled service for an individually ticketed passenger. When used to perform any group tour service, the same vehicle is called a motor coach.

Cancellation

A reservation voided at the guest's request. This can be for one guest room, a meal function or even an entire group's activities.

CRT or (Cathode Ray Tube)

An output device of a computer system, which is usually capable of displaying both text and graphics. Also called a monitor, a display screen, or simply a screen.

Cash Bar .

A private room bar setup where guests pay for their drinks. These are sometimes called a COD bar or an a la carte bar and there is usually a minimum level of revenue that must be reached to avoid a service charge by the hotel.

Casino Hotel

A hotel with gaming facilities. Many also have elaborate restaurants, lounges, entertainment centers and meeting spaces. These are restricted by strict legal definitions to locations where gaming is allowed.

Central Reservations Office (CRO)

Part of an affiliate reservation network. A central reservations office typically deals directly with the public, advertises a central (usually toll-free) telephone number, provides participating properties with necessary communications equipment, and bills properties for handling reservations. They may also be called Central Reservation Services, especially if they represent independent operators or more than one brand.

Channels of Distribution

The methods by which sellers reach potential buyers. Travel agents, tour operators, tour wholesalers and Internet referral and link options are part of this system within the tourism industry.

Charter

To hire the exclusive use of any aircraft, vessel, bus, limo or other vehicle that is usually driven or piloted by someone else.

Check-In

A hotel property day starts at 6 a.m.; however, occupancy of rooms by arriving guests may not be possible until after the established checkout time (usually around 12 noon).

Check Out (verb)

To vacate a room, taking luggage, turning in key card and paying bill

Check-out (noun)

A room that a guest has officially vacated. Check-out time is usually between 11 am and 12 noon.

Circulation Broadcast Advertising

The number of set owning homes within the station's coverage area. This is a factor in measuring television or cable audience.

City Ledger

A term from pre-computerized days when local accounts were billed in the "city" and kept as a separate "ledger". Today, these are folios of guests who have checked out or local business firms with approval from the manager for direct billing.

Closed Dates

Dates on which rooms cannot be sold because of a "full-house," or all rooms are pre-reserved or already occupied.

Closed to arrival

Dates that arrivals are no longer desirable, as they would prevent guests who want to stay longer from being able to do so. This is a yield or revenue management strategy.

Closet count

The amount of linen in the room attendant's closet.

Cold Call

A fact finding mission in making contacts to determine if the client has any business potential for your hotel. They are often viewed incorrectly as only an outside sales call to a new client without an appointment. In fact, cold calls can be made in person or by phone.

Commission Payment

The percentage of room rate paid to travel agencies for their bookings. (Usually 10%, sometimes negotiated either up or down)

Complimentary Room (Comp)

A room free of charge, approved by management or the sales staff.

Commercial or Corporate Hotel

A property, usually located in a downtown or business district, that caters primarily to business clients. Their services may include a business center, overnight delivery locations, business class accommodations and other amenities targeting corporate travelers.

Commercial or Corporate Rate

A special room rate, lower than rack rate, agreed upon by a hotel and a company. Some hotels offer these at a slight discount to anyone on request. Others have negotiated corporate rates that may be lower or that offer more services, preferred availability or upgraded accommodations in exchange for guaranteed volumes of rooms used during a certain time period. These may be negotiated locally or through a brand's national sales offices.

Commissionable Rate

The special rate a hotel or other facility quotes, which the hotel or facility will pay a commission to agents or other third party intermediary that referred the business.

Commissions

are forms of compensation paid to travel agents or wholesalers for referring of business directly to a hotel. There are chain or private settlement services that provides monthly-centralized commission checks for all bookings made by participating travel agencies with member hotel organizations. These streamlined payment processes make it quicker for hotels to pay their commissions due, which in turn gives the agencies continued incentives to refer their clients who are satisfied with the hotels' services and offerings.

Competition Analysis

An evaluation of a business's competition to identify opportunities and unique selling points. Part of a marketing audit and the annual marketing plan, it analyzes the strengths and weaknesses of each competitor from the guests' viewpoint.

Competitive Set

This a grouping of competitors that compete regularly in many or most market segments. For example, Four Seasons Hotels do not regularly compete with Days Inns, but with Ritz-Carlton, St. Regis and upscale Hyatts. Many, but not all, Best Western hotels compete with Hampton Inns, Holiday Express and Comfort Inns, while others may compete with brands that are slightly higher or lower in rate and service/product offerings, such as Marriott Courtyard, Four Points or Super 8. Knowing your own competitive set can be essential to maintaining proper marketplace positioning and market share.

Complimentary Room

A complimentary or "comp" room is a room that is occupied, but the guest is not charged for its use and is "free". A hotel may offer comp rooms to a group in ratio to the total number of rooms the group occupies. One comp room may be offered for each twenty rooms occupied, for example. Rooms may be provided on a complimentary basis for someone looking at using your hotel in the future for a group

Concierge

A hotel employee whose task is to serve as the guest's liaison with hotel and non-hotel attractions, facilities, services, and activities. This person often arranges for tickets to sporting or theatrical events, makes reservations at restaurants and handles unusual requests for hotel guests.

Conducted Tour

A prearranged travel program, usually for a group, which includes an escort for the entire length of the program or a single portion of sightseeing program conducted by a guide, such as a city tour. Also called an escorted tour.

Conference

A meeting or assembly of employees from the same company gathering at a hotel or conference center for a common purpose.

Conference Center

A property specifically designed to handle group meetings. Conference centers are often located outside metropolitan areas, near universities or recreational centers. They may provide extensive meeting and leisure facilities. Although they try to offer more private settings. Most offer overnight accommodations and serve American Plan food service (three meals per day).

Confirmation

A written notice to guest in advance of arrival that room has been reserved. Today, most hotels use only confirmation numbers that are automatically generated by their computer.

Connecting Rooms

Adjacent rooms with a connecting door in between, these rooms are most desirable for families with small children.

Continental Breakfast

A term used to describe a light breakfast that frequently includes juice, coffee (or tea) and some kind of bakery item, such as a bagel or muffin. The range of offerings widely varies and some have expanded to include fresh fruit, cereals and elaborate set-ups, while others are very basic and may only include donuts or toast. Some hotels provide these with their room charge, while others charge a fee.

Convention

An assembly of association attendees gathering for a common purpose, usually including meetings, banquets, and room accommodations.

Convention Center

A facility specifically designed to handle large group or specialty meetings. Many convention centers are often located inside both large and smaller metropolitan areas and may be partially built with lodging or other locally generated taxes. They may cater to larger meetings or to a mix of business that includes local shows and events. Most try to have a hotel attached to the center as a service and a generator of business for the convention center. There are some very large hotels that have self-contained convention centers, such as the Opryland Hotel in Nashville, the Anatole Plaza in Dallas and many properties that have gaming affiliations.

Day Rate (Also called Day Use)

Renting room for part of day, normally mid morning to mid or late afternoon. These are often used by business travelers with late international flights or by people who need to use their room as an office. Rates (frequently in the 50% range) and specifics policies are determined by local management. These rooms can be used in the day, cleaned and then resold that evening, increasing revenue and REVPAR for the day.

Deposit

A monetary payment to property by guest in advance of arrival to assure room will be held. These are frequently requested for special events or periods of excess demand.

Desk Information Book

Contains information that needs to be used for reference and/or to give local information to visitors and guests. This often contains sample menus, brochures and maps.

Destination

In the travel industry, any city, area, or country that can be marketed as a single entity to tourists. Examples include:

- Branson, Missouri
- Disney World
- New York City
- New Orleans
- Grand Canyon
- Niagara Falls
- Yellowstone or Yosemite National Parks

Differentiation

A critical marketing strategy designed to emphasize the unique selling points of a business and the differences between that business and its competitors.

Direct Flight

A journey on which the passenger does not have to change planes. Not necessarily non-stop.

Direct Mail Advertising

Advertising mailed to the consumer's residence or office, containing copy that tries to motivate the reader to purchase a product or utilize a service. The most successful programs contain a response mechanism for ordering by return mail, the Internet or phone.

Discount Rates

Pre-determined special rates provided to certain market segments such as seniors, government, etc. They may be promoted as a percentage discounted from rack rates or as a specific quoted rate.

Discounting

Marking down the normal room rates by some percentage or dollar amount. Discounts are usually directed toward particular markets or are instituted during a particular time or season. They are only effective if they drive "new" business to your hotel.

Distressed Passenger

A passenger on an airline, or other mode of public transportation that has been displaced (or delayed) due to weather, "acts of God", or mechanical failure on the part of the carrier. Distressed passengers are normally given vouchers to stay and eat at a hotel, that is reimbursed by the carrier to the hotel.

Direct Bill

An account that has been approved by the manager and to which the property will send a bill after check-out. The guest at check-out must sign the folio.

Discards

Linen or other articles too badly worn, torn, stained or burned to be used for guests.

DND (Do Not Disturb)

Abbreviation indicating that the guest does not want his/her room to be entered nor does he/she wants to be disturbed.

Double (Occupancy)

A room to be occupied by two people.

Double-Double

A room with two double beds, these are most frequently in demand by families and tour groups.

Double Occupancy Rate

A rate used where the "per person" charge is based on two to a room. Some hotels use this as a way to boost revenues, while others charge a per room rate.

Double-locked

Guest room door is bolted from the inside and cannot be opened with a key card. Before knocking on any guest room door, the housekeeping staff must first test the door lock button that indicates if the door is double-locked.

Drop Cloth

Heavy clothe used by workmen to protect furniture and carpets.

Due Out

1. The day when a room is expected to be vacated.

2. A room that is expected to be vacated on that day.

Economy hotels

See Budget hotels

Efficiency

Accommodations containing some type of kitchen facility.

Escort

A person, usually employed by a tour operator, who accompanies a tour either from departure to return or in a single location such as a city or national park. They also assist the bus driver by serving as a guide and trouble-shooter.

Executive Floor

A floor of a hotel that offers exceptional and additional services to business and other travelers who are paying a premium rate. These are also called a business floor, concierge level or The Towers.

Extended Stay hotels

Accommodations that blend the offerings of all suite hotels and efficiencies in a variation of an apartment setting. This segment targets people who may be seeking longer term accommodations for reasons that may include relocation or long term assignments. Many of them offer varying degrees of limited housekeeping service.

European Plan

A room rate that does not include any meals.

Familiarization Tour

A complimentary or reduced-rate travel program. A familiarization or "fam" tour is designed to acquaint travel agents, meeting planners, travel writers, and others with a specific destination or destinations and stimulate sales. Convention and visitors' bureaus or national brand sales offices often arrange these.

Family Rate

A special room rate for families using the same guest room, that does not charge extra for children under a certain age.

Feeder City/Market

A city/area other than the property's city/area from which guests arrive. This information can be obtained from your central reservation office's data banks or from your own hotel's property management system.

Flat Rate

A specific room rate for a group, agreed upon by the hotel and the group in advance. A flat rate is the same rate, regardless of the room type or number of people that occupy the room, up to the legal limit.

This is also called a "run of the house" rate.

Flyer

A printed, low-cost advertisement intended for distribution to potential clients or guests, usually by mail.

Folio

A printed financial statement of all guest or group transactions recapping the activity and remaining balance of a single account.

Forecast

Future projection of estimated business volume. The general manager, sales manager and front office/reservations manager, as applicable to size of hotel, should review these at least weekly.

Action steps should be planned and taken. Forecasting is a moving target and should be updated from the annual budget forecast. A 90 day update is essential weekly to monitor unexpected demand or shortfall. Larger hotels frequently will review up to 180 days weekly.

Paying attention to developing trends will allow the hotel to be able to serve the maximum number of guests profitably, while insuring that rates and availability offer guests the maximum in options.

Front Desk

The focal point of activity within the hotel, usually prominently located in the hotel lobby. Guests are registered, assigned rooms, and checked out at the front desk. Regardless of the size of hotel, the desk is the center of communication for all guests. The desk is where key cards are kept, mail and messages are distributed and from which information is dispensed to both guests and staff.

Front Desk Agent/Receptionist

Formerly called "clerk", this is a hotel employee whose responsibilities center on the registration process, but also typically includes pre-registration activities, room status coordination, and mail, messages and information requests. These agents are key to effective sales tactics, such as Upselling and gathering of leads for referral to the sales team.

Front Desk Cashier

Person who verifies all charges made to a room and collects money upon departure of guests. At many smaller properties, the desk agent handles both the check-in and check-out process.

Front of the House

The functional areas of the hotel in which employees have extensive guest contact, such as restaurants, lounges, meeting space and the front office.

Full Comp

No charges made for room, meals taken in property, telephone, valet or any items. These require management approval and are usually provided only for the head of large groups who bring substantial business to the hotel.

Function Book

The master control of all banquet space, broken down on each page by banquet rooms and restaurants, with a page for each day of the year. Proper use of this inventory can mean serving more guests comfortably and profitably. Much of this is contained on computer databases at many hotels today.

Gateway City

A city with an airport and/or seaport that handles direct flights or cruises from other countries. In the US and Canada, a partial list would include:

- Boston
- New York
- Washington, DC
- Atlanta
- Miami
- Orlando
- New Orleans
- Dallas

- Houston
- Chicago
- LA
- San Francisco
- San Diego
- Halifax
- Montreal
- Toronto
- Vancouver

GDS (Global Distribution System)

An Internet based interconnecting network of systems used by travel agents and certain other wholesalers to book airline, auto, hotel, cruises and other hospitality services and products. These websites are usually linked to each other and there is normally a handling or connection fee associated to the service provider, such as a hotel.

Government Rate

A special room rate made available at some properties for government employees. Federal rates are set nationally in the US and Canada, with premiums set for cities acknowledged as being high cost of living and that respective government establishes state or Canadian provincial rates. In both cases, government travelers are not reimbursed for more than the per diem (rate per day) for food and accommodations and will seldom use properties that charge more. It can be a sales advantage to include breakfast for this market, as the individual can apply that meal's credit to another service. Some hotels package meeting space or breaks into the rate, in exchange for certain volumes of business or at certain times of the year.

Ground Operator

A company or individual providing such services as hotel accommodations, sightseeing, transfers, and other related services, within a given destination. These are sometimes called a purveyor or destination management companies.

Group Code

Group name on folio under rate information, used for tracking pick-up of groups and of evaluating certain market demand.

Group Rate

A special room rate for a number of affiliated guests. This rate is usually, but not always a discounted rate. Instead of a discount room rate, it could include other packaged services, such as a meal, recreational privileges or other amenities.

Group Reservation

A specified minimum number of reservations of rooms handled by the sales department for a particular group.

Guarantee

Figure given by a function planner to the property, usually at least 48 hours prior to a function, stating number of persons o be served -

Guaranteed Reservation (GTD)

An agreement between a property and a guest when a company,   travel agent or person guarantees payment for accommodations and the property agrees to hold the reservation all night. A credit card number or company name and address are the most common forms of guarantee.

Guaranteed No-show (GTD-NS)

When a person with a guaranteed reservation (see above) does not arrive at the property and does not cancel before the specified time, the property will bill one night's lodging charges to the company or the credit card.

Guest Charge

Anything on guest's bill – room charges, purchases, room service, telephone, valet, etc.

Guest Folio

See folio.

Guarantee

The figure which a function or meeting planner gives to the hotel at least 24 to 48 hours before the function for the number of persons to be served.

Most hotels are prepared to serve 5% to 10% over the guaranteed figure. Payment is made on the basis of the guaranteed number of covers or the total number served, whichever is greater. Payment is usually covered by a combination of an advance deposit with the balance paid at the time of service, unless it is a regular client or with approved credit.

Guaranteed Reservation

A reservation which assures the guest that a room will be held until checkout time of the day following the day of arrival. The guest guarantees payment for the room, even if it is not used, unless the reservation is properly canceled. Types of guaranteed reservations include pre-payment, credit card, advance deposit, travel agent, and company approved credit.

Guest History (card or computer memory)

A record of the guest's visits that might include company, personal accommodation preferences, method of payment, rooms assigned, rates, special needs, frequent traveler numbers and other information. This is an essential marketing tool, as it identifies repeat guests and potential related business. For regular travelers, this is a personalized service that is most appreciated. For the hotel, it is a sales and marketing tactic that meets the strategy of building a base of repeat customers. Almost all property management systems today have a variation of this feature, which is based on the manual system of noting and using the guest's preferences on index cards.

Guest Mix

The variety and percentage distribution of hotel guests: individual, group, business, leisure, etc. This is important to track, as sales and marketing efforts are frequently directed to those with known usage and/or potential. Understanding and addressing the mix of business can assist in both maximizing revenues and in serving the best mix of guests for your hotel.

Guest Room Control (book or computer data base)

A resource used to monitor the number of guest rooms committed to groups. It is essential this be regularly updated, as availability may be dramatically altered if the groups exceed or fall short of their commitments.

Heavy Clean

A rooms division term used to indicate a very thorough cleaning of a guest room and bath. This is done on a periodic basis and will likely include carpet shampooing, dry cleaning of curtains, and possible touch up painting and extensive cleaning to keep the accommodation fresh.

Heavy Vacuuming

Vacuuming an area thoroughly, which includes moving furniture and vacuuming behind it.

High Balance

Report prepared for night audit to notify Front Office Manager of guests whose folio balances have exceeded established limits.

Hold for Arrival

Mail and packages, etc. arriving prior to arrival of guest. "Hold for Arrival" and expected date is noted on article.

Hospitality (Room)

A room used for entertaining, i.e. cocktail party, etc. and may be either a function room or parlor.

Hospitality Suite

A parlor with connecting bedroom(s) to be used for entertaining.

Host Bar

A private room bar setup with drinks prepaid by the host or sponsor. This is sometimes called a sponsored bar.

Hotel Representative

An individual or company who offers hotel reservations to wholesalers, travel agents, and the public. A hotel representative or "rep" may be paid by the hotels he or she represents on a fee basis or by commission. Many hotel reps also offer marketing and other services and work primarily with larger groups.

Hotel Sales & Marketing Association International (HSMAI)

A professional society of hotel salespeople, managers, owners, and other sales-minded hotel executives, dedicated to the further education of its members. HSMAI conducts seminars, clinics, workshops, an annual convention, and publishes a quarterly magazine, HSMAI Marketing Review, as well as books and pamphlets on hospitality sales.

Housekeeping operational codes

OCC. (Occupied): A guest room in which a guest or the guest's belongings are present.

VAC. (Vacant): A guest room that is ready to be sold to a new guest.

M.U. (Make-Up or Stay Over): A guest room that needs to be cleaned, including fresh linens.

OCC. M.U: (Occupied Make-Up): A guest room that is occupied and is a make-up.

P.O. (Pick Up): A vacant guest room that requires minor attention before it is ready   for a new guest.

S.O. (Sleep Out): Refers to a guest room that is occupied but not slept in.

Reocc. (Reoccupied): Refers to a room that was a checkout earlier in the day and is   now occupied by a new guest.

OOO: (Out of Order): Guest room is not sellable.

Housekeeping Reports

Reports turned in to Front Desk by Housekeeping late in afternoon and used to verify that Housekeeping and Front Desk show same status on rooms' inventory as vacant, vacant dirty, occupied, or occupied dirty.

House Count

How many rooms have been sold for that night.

HSK.

Abbreviation for Housekeeping Department.

Incentive Travel

Travel financed by a business as an employee incentive. While most incentive destinations tend to be resorts or more exotic locations, there is the potential for different types of properties to tie into at least a portion of this market.

Inclusive Tour

A tour in which specific elements - airfare, hotels, transfers, etc. - is included for a flat rate. An inclusive tour rate does not necessarily cover all costs such as shopping, certain gratuities, etc.

Independent Hotel

A hotel with no chain or franchise affiliation, although one hotel owner might own several such properties.

Information Rack

Revolving rack at desk or central telephone (formerly called PBX) with all guest information slips filed alphabetically. Computerized systems have eliminated many of these kinds of manual racks.

Inspected

Room has been thoroughly checked by a housekeeping supervisor or manager.

Inventory

1. In sales and front office management, it is the total count of all accommodations available on a given date and how they might be allocated to groups, discounts, or certain other criteria

2 In food & beverage, it refers to the stock of food and liquors in storage and in the process of being used

3. In housekeeping, it is the cumulative total of all linens in use, in storage or in the laundry

Junior (or mini) Suite

An oversized room, usually with a partition separating the bedroom furnishings from the sitting area.

Key card Control

A security system requiring each employee to account for all key cards used during working hours. Most hotels changed from metal keys to electronic locks in the 1990s for improved security and accountability.

Key card Drawer/key card Area

Where key cards are stored. Drawer or cabinet should be locked when cabinet is not in use.

King

Largest size bed available from manufacturers, usually 72-80" wide; older hotels used to form temporary "kings" by putting two twin mattresses crosswise on twin box springs.

Late Service Room

A room that requires service after the end of the day shift.

Letter of Agreement

A document listing services, space, pricing and products that becomes binding when signed by both parties. This is usually for company guaranteed programs for individual rooms business and for group, meeting and banquet business.

Linen Closet

Located on each guest floor and contains linen and supplies necessary to service the guest rooms.

Linen Room/Laundry Room

Central area of the Housekeeping Department from which all key cards, uniforms, supplies and linen are issued. The Linen Room is also the communication center for the House-keeping Department.

Local Rate

A rate the media offers to local advertisers, which is lower than the national rate.

Lock-out

Locking a guest out of the room for non-payment for services already rendered. The guest cannot get into the room until he or she speaks with the manager.

Log Book – front desk

Daily diary where special instructions are noted for follow up and/or documentation.

Log Book(s) – housekeeping/laundry

The Linen Room Supervisor or Attendant records a record in the Linen Room in which all calls, requests and other important information.

Logo

The name of a company or product in a special design used as a trademark. These are all protected by law and cannot be changed or copied. The colors, shape and design must all be consistent with the standards.

Lost and Found

While normally handled by housekeeping, this area of responsibility must be properly maintained in handling any items that are found or alleged to have been lost.

Mailing List

A list of the names, addresses, and, in some cases, titles of persons to be reached by direct mail. It can be a commercial, general, or house list. Hotels can generate their own list from their property management system or other resources, such as banquet or meetings customers.

Make-up/Stay Over

Change linen on beds, clean room and bathroom while guest is registered in room.

Manager on Duty (M.O.D.)

Usually a regularly assigned manager or a designated department head, this person assumes full responsibility for the property in the absence of the General Manager.

Market

A geographic area defined by media coverage or sales patterns. This also refers to a population group that has purchasing power and is a prime prospect for an advertiser's product or service.

Marketing

A system of interacting activities formulated to plan, price, promote, and make available services or products to potential customers or guests in a particular target market.

Marketing Mix

The combination of the four "Ps" of marketing used to achieve marketing objectives for a target market.

The four "Ps" are:

- Product
- Price
- Place
- Promotion

Marketplace Analysis

An evaluation of the environmental trends and forces affecting a business, such as changes in lifestyles and societal values, economic conditions, and technology. Part of a situation analysis, this is an important component of the planning process as it provides an objective overview of what is happening in your marketplace.

Market Research

The use of various techniques to obtain data on past and potential customers or guests. Used by a business to improve its marketing and sales effectiveness, it can anticipate changes or trends in guest preferences.

Market Segmentation

Dividing the market into groups of consumers with similar needs, wants, backgrounds, incomes, buying habits, and so on. Regardless of the type of hotel or location you have, this is essential to note changes in demand, price flexibility or sensitivity in the various kinds of guests you serve. Unless you serve only one type of customer, such as a military restricted property, understanding the trends and needs of your market segments is essential to long-term success.

Market Share

The amount of a market a business captures relative to the total market.

Master Account

One folio prepared for a group on which all group charges are accumulated. Also called a master folio, a particular brand may also use this term as an internal service.

Master Bucket

Contains internal and master folios.

Master Card or Data Base

An index that contains a summary of everything needed for a sales effort, including the organization's name, the decision-maker(s), key contacts, addresses, telephone numbers, and so on.

MAP (Modified American Plan)

A room rate that includes two meals-typically breakfast and dinner. These are used primarily at resorts and some conference center hotels.

Motor coach

A large highway passenger vehicle used to perform any travel service other than scheduled transportation for individually ticketed passengers. Contains such passenger comfort items as climate control, carpeting, reclining seats, pillow service, etc.

MTD

Month to date - these are the accounting totals showing the revenues and expenditures for a specific month as of a specific date.

National Tour Association

A trade association of U.S. motor coach operators federally licensed by the Interstate Commerce Commission with the purpose of promoting member professionalism and motor coach tour development. Many hotels and attractions belong as allied members to network, seek business and network with tour operators.

Net Rate

Non-commissionable rate. Some travel agents are now beginning to use net rates and adding service fees to their clients or packaging differently.

Night Auditor

Person who balances property accounts and posts all guest charges on bills. Normal shift is 11 PM – 7 AM.

No Baggage

Possibly day occupancy or a prepaid account.

No Show, Employee

An employee who does not come to work when scheduled and who does not call in to report absenteeism or tardiness.

No Show, Guest

1. A passenger or guest who fails either to use or cancel his or her reservation

2. A reservation neither canceled nor fulfilled.

There are certain legal procedures that must be followed to collect on these,

O/C

Occupied with baggage.

Occupancy

Percentage of number of rooms actually in use, divided by number of rooms available to rent.

Occupancy & Activity Analysis

An analysis of a property's past, present, and potential operating statistics. Some of the information is gathered from the daily business summary or night auditor's report, but the total analysis should be included as detailed portion of the situation analysis in order to accurately assess trends.

On Change

Room vacant but not yet reported by housekeeper as clean. Status of a guest room, not rentable because it is being repaired or redecorated.

Ontario Motor Coach Tour Association

A trade association of Canadian motor coach operators federally licensed with the purpose of promoting member professionalism and motor coach tour development. Many hotels and attractions belong as allied members to network, seek business and network with tour operators.

Open

The availability of rooms for sale.

Operation

The active functioning of property, especially activities, dealing directly with serving guests.

Option Date

The prearranged date by which a tentative agreement between a buyer and seller must become a definite agreement or become void.

Out of Order

Rooms that cannot be occupied by guests, due to physical reason like painting, defective plumbing, etc.

Overbooking

Committing more rooms than are actually available to ensure the highest guest occupancy, taking into consideration cancellations and no-shows from occupancy tracking history. This is not a recommended activity, as there may be serious legal complications.

Oversold

Reservations have been accepted beyond a property's capacity to provide rooms.

Overstay

A guest who stays after his or her stated departure date. (Note: most states and provinces have laws that deal with overstays, even if another guest books the room for that evening. One way to address the issue is to circle the agreed upon departure date and have the guest initial it at check-in. This is a sensitive legal issue that you should research in your home state/province for direction. Your state/provincial hotel association is an excellent resource)

Outdoor Advertising

A location on a busy interstate or heading into a large metropolitan area will cost more to use based on traffic counts as the number of people passing an advertisement with an opportunity to view it.

Package

A special offering of products and services created by a hotel to increase sales. There are weekend packages, honeymoon packages, sports packages, and so on. A typical package might include the guest room, meals, and use of the property's recreational facilities for a special price. Options might be auto rentals, admission to area attractions, etc.

Packager

An individual or organization coordinating and promoting the development of a package tour and establishing operating procedures and guidelines for the tour.

Package Tour

A salable travel product, which offers, at an inclusive price, several travel elements, which a traveler would otherwise purchase separately. A package tour can include, in varying degrees, any or all of the following elements:

- lodging
- sight-seeing
- admission to certain attractions
- selected meals
- live entertainment
- car rental and
- transportation by air, motor coach, rail, or even private vehicle. A package tour may include more than one destination.

Painted Display

An outdoor advertisement painted on a billboard or wall that is usually illuminated. (see billboard)

Par

Number of sets of linen needed per bed or sets of towels per guest.

Parlor

A sitting room that may or may not have a bathroom or sleeping accommodations.

Peak Period

Also known as "in-season, or high season", this is the period when demand for a property and its services is highest. Maximum rates are usually charged at this time, along with some additional premiums such as setting minimum lengths of reservations, pre-payment, accepting only certain arrival days, etc.

Personal Selling

A method of securing business through direct personal contact with potential clients or guests. It is common to all brands and all locations.

Plant

The entire property operation

Point-of-Purchase

Tent cards, elevator promotions, posters, displays, and other materials placed in prominent areas of the hotel to influence buying decisions.

Positioning Materials

A marketing term used to describe how consumers perceive the products and services offered by a particular hotel in relation to similar products and services offered by competitors. Positioning strategies attempt to establish in the minds of consumers a particular image of a hotel's products and services.

Pre-block

Assigning a specific room or suite number prior to actual arrival date of guest

Pre-registration

A process by which sections of a registration card or its equivalent are completed for guests arriving with reservations. Room and rate assignment, creation of a guest folio, and other functions may also be part of pre-registration activity. It speeds the check-in process considerably, especially in hotels with heavy periods of registration.

Print Advertising

Costs can vary for advertising based on the number of copies sold or distributed by the publication, which can include magazines, directories, newspapers, catalogues, or travel industry promotional materials.

Property

The building, land, and all facilities connected with a hotel facility.

Property Department in hotel

Often a division of housekeeping in a large hotel that does heavy maintenance cleaning in front and back of house and usually includes the night (3rd shift) cleaning crew,. This department may also be in charge of keeping up exteriors and grounds.

Property Analysis

A realistic evaluation of a business's facilities, services, and programs to determine its strengths and weaknesses. Part of a marketing audit, it analyzes the strengths and weaknesses from the guests' viewpoint.

Publicity

The gratuitous mention in the media of an organization's people, products, or services. Publicity can be positive, such as in receiving an award, or negative in a situation that highlights a fire or a case of alleged food poisoning. Relationships with the local media can often be the difference in how a story is communicated to the community.

Public Relations (PR)

A systematic effort by a business to communicate favorable information about itself to the public in order to create a positive impression. The involvement of an owner, manager or sales representative in community affairs often provides a positive identity of your hotel in the minds of people who live and work in your community.

Qualify

The act of determining if a prospect has a need for or can afford the products and services offered by a property. All markets are not desirable or accessible to all hotels; for example, a five star hotel does typically not cater to youth tours and a roadside one-diamond property will not seek association business even if they are in a capital city.

Queen

A room with a queen sized bed. Queen sized beds are smaller than a king and larger than a double bed. Some hotels feature rooms with two queen beds as a selling point.

Rack Rate

The regular retail selling prices of accommodations as established by management. Special events may increase rack rates. In many US states and Canadian provinces, maximum rates must be posted visibly in the guest room.

Register

The guest check-in procedure.

Relocate or Walk

Guest accommodated at another hotel because property was unable to honor his reservation.

Reservation

Advance request for a room.

Reservation Card

Special reservation request form printed for specific conventions that are mailed to the hotel. These are usually used at large convention hotels in major cities.

Revenue Management

Also known as yield management, the goals of revenue management are to maximize revenues and serve the greatest number of guests, regardless of demand. Revenue management is not specifically raising or lowering prices, but is a management tool to improve profitability. The airlines began computerized yield management in the 1980s, although there were a number of successful hoteliers who understood and used the principles of revenue management in the 1960s and 1970s. Strategies may include tactics such as:

• setting or eliminating minimum lengths of reservations

• pre-payment

• accepting only certain arrival days, etc.

• requiring that all reservations are guaranteed

• increasing or limiting certain discounts

Most brand hotels have programs or workshops to assist you in refining your personal approach to revenue management, as it requires an ongoing commitment by management and sales to be effective. Contact your brand's training department, the Educational Institute of AH&LA, HSMAI or one of the other resources available mentioned elsewhere in this book for additional information on revenue management.

Rollaway

A portable bed, usually twin sized, that is available for an additional person staying in a room.

Roll in/Roll out

Put rollaway bed in or remove from the guest room.

Rack Rate

The standard, retail rate established by a property for a particular category of rooms. This the rate on which all discounts is based. The term comes from the background that hotels used to have all of their room numbers mounted on a physical rack behind the front desk and the staff would assign rooms based on availability noted on the rack. Computers have eliminated most racks.

Rate Card

A printed listing of rates and general information about the hotel. Many hotels use cards to promote specialty markets, such as welcome centers, weekend packages, special occasion plans like weddings, reunions, etc. These can be very cost effective.

Reciprocal Advertising

The exchange of an advertiser's products or services to pay for all or part of the medium's time or space. Also called due bill advertising or barter, these agreements are sometimes arranged through management or national sales offices.

Registration Card

A printed form the guest completes upon arrival, giving name, address, method of payment, agreed upon room rate, departure date and other information. It is important that guests sign this card at check in to confirm the above information from a legal perspective, as the final acknowledgment of the contractual agreement between guest and hotel.

Reservation

An agreement between a hotel and a guest that the hotel will hold a specific type of room for a particular date and length of stay in exchange for the guest's promise to pay the agreed upon rate. This is in fact a legal and potentially binding contract.

Reservations Agent

An employee, either in the front office, in a separate department or conceivably in a reservations center, who is responsible for all aspects of reservations processing.

Reservation Traffic Statistical Reports

These vary by chain or reservation referral source, but they are valuable tools for hotels of all sizes in any location because most provide personalized information about your hotel. This may include:

- number of reservations processed through the CRO
- number of nights relating to the reservations from the CRO
- confirmed rates and total estimated room revenue
- zip code or area code of referral
- company name of person booking reservation
- number of reservation requests declined by the guest by category (rate, location, did not have desired room type, etc.)
- number of reservations denied due to no availability listed in the CRO service.

Matching this data with your performance on those dates can be invaluable in improving your performance. It can also be an excellent resource to prospect for future potential clients.

Resort Hotel

A hotel that provides scenery and recreational activities unavailable at most other properties. Guests are more typically vacationers or people perhaps combining meetings with personal time before or after their business obligations.

Retail Travel Agent

An individual qualified to arrange and sell lodging, transportation and other travel services and products directly to the public.

RevPAR

Revenue per Available Room is an industry term that became relevant in the 1990s as a measurement tool more accurate than only occupancy and ADR (average daily rate). RevPAR multiplies those two statistics to identify a measurement that assesses the overall success of all available rooms, not just those rented. RevPAR will always be lower than ADR except when 100% occupancy is achieved.

RevPAC

Revenue per Available Customer goes one step further than RevPAR in analyzing the statistical impact of the individual customer. It includes the counting of guests in each room and applying that multiple occupancy factor in assessing the contribution of each guest to the hotel's revenue stream. This is used particularly by casinos, resorts and large convention hotels that have substantial revenue centers in addition to rooms, such as gaming, golf, tennis, shopping, equipment rental, banquets and meetings, that closely calculate the total value of each guest in financial terms.

Rifle Approach

To concentrate sales or marketing efforts on narrowly defined targets, such as a specific market in a certain season.

Room Attendant Cart

A vehicle that carries linen, supplies and equipment required by the Room Attendant to service four guest rooms at a time. One cart is assigned to each section.

Room Block

An agreed-upon number of rooms set aside for members of a group planning to stay at a hotel. The group commits to using the reserved rooms and the hotel commits to making them available. This could also be a specific room "blocked" or reserved for a particular guest on a certain day.

Room Board/rack

A piece of Front Office equipment representing the guest rooms in the form of metal pockets in which colors and symbols identify the accommodations. Computerized systems have eliminated many of these kinds of manual racks.

Room Change

Guest changing from one room to another.

Room Revenue Report

Report made out by 3 p.m.-11 p.m. clerks showing number of occupants and revenue received for each occupied room. Computerized systems have eliminated many of these kinds of manual reports.

Room Rate

The price a hotel charges for overnight accommodations.

Room Status

Availability of guest rooms for sale, i.e., ready, check out, etc.

Rooming

Escorting guest to assigned room.

Rooming List

A list of guests who will occupy reserved accommodations participating in a group reservation block, submitted by the buyer in advance. This is used most frequently by tours, youth groups, teams and certain company sponsored events.

ROP Color

In newspaper advertising, this is color used in regular sections of the paper and printed on standard newsprint.

Run of the House Rate

A flat rate per room regardless of the room type or number of people occupying a room.

Sales Promotions

Promotional activities that are neither personal selling nor media advertising. Sales promotions may include :
- offering free samples
- discount coupons

• staging contests, exhibits, or displays
• attending trade shows.

Sales Support

Materials used to assist in selling, such as printed brochures, endorsement letters, materials, charts, video brochures, and posters.

Section

A group of rooms on one floor that equal s one Room Attendant's room quota.

Sofa Bed

Sofa that opens into a bed.

Security

The department (or personnel) that is in charge of protecting property, employees, and guests from thefts and vandalism.

Self-mailer

Direct mail literature that folds up to make its own envelope.

Selling Up

Making an effort to sell the better, higher rated room.

Sell Out/Sold Out

All available rooms reserved or occupied on a specific date.

Sell Through

Accepting reservations for multiple nights through sold out dates to increase occupancy on open dates

Service Charge

A percentage of the bill (usually 15% to 20%) added for distribution to service employees in lieu of direct tipping. These are usually part of group banquets and sometimes used for organized groups or tours for housekeepers, bell staff and/or front desk.

Share (or Share With)

A guest who joins another guest already occupying a room at a property (non-family).

Shotgun Approach

To spread sales or marketing efforts broadly over the marketplace, not necessarily targeting any special groups of potential clients.

Shoulder Period

This is a period when the level of business for a property falls somewhere between its peak and valley periods.

Single

Room to be occupied by one person, regardless of bed type.

Situation Analysis

A comprehensive evaluation of a business's current position in the marketplace. An integral part of a marketing audit, it gives hoteliers an objective overview of the marketplace.

Skips

Guests who leave the property without paying the bill.

Sleepers

Rooms not physically occupied (possibly skips) and not discovered by desk during the course of the day, therefore, room not rented due to account still being active.

Sleep-Out

A room in which the guest did not sleep in the bed, but still pays for it.

Spotting

Used to describe removal of stains on a limited surface.

Standard

A measurement one column wide by one inch deep. National newspaper Advertising Unit and magazine advertising is often quoted in terms of SAUs.

Stay-over

A room status term indicating that the guest is not checking out and will remain at least one more night.

Storyboard

A series of drawings illustrating the characters, action, and dialogue of a proposed television commercial, or plan of action.

Studio

A small room with one (double bed) and a couch.

Suggestive Selling

The practice of influencing a guest's purchase decision through the use of sales phrases.

Suite

Two or more rooms with a sitting area, bathroom and sleeping area that can be closed off from each other with a door.

Suite Hotel

A hotel whose entire inventory of sleeping accommodations are rooms that have separate bedroom, bathroom, living room or parlor areas, and perhaps a kitchenette or other special features.

Tabloid

A newspaper smaller than a standard newspaper.

Target Markets

Market segments that a property identifies as having the greatest potential, and toward which marketing activities are aimed.

Test Marketing

The testing of a marketing or media concept in a selected market or markets an advertising campaign conducted in conjunction with research tools to determine the advisability of extending a marketing program to a broader area of the country.

Tidy-Up

To straighten and clean a room after guest's departure when full service has been given earlier.

Toilet Tissue

Toilet paper - not to be confused with facial tissue - placed for convenience of guest in bathrooms or public lavatories.

Tour

Any prearranged (but not necessarily prepaid) journey to one or more places and back to the point of origin.

Tour Broker

An individual licensed and bonded by the Interstate Commerce Commission to operate motor coach tours in the United States and, in some cases, Canada, as permitted by the scope of his or her license. Also known as a motor coach broker or tour operator.

Tour Voucher

A document issued by tour brokers to be exchanged for accommodations, meals, sightseeing, and other services. Sometimes called coupons.

Tour Wholesaler

An individual who puts tour packages together, usually involving air transportation.

Trace Card

A 3- by 5-inch index card used as a reminder to call a client or check a cut-off date, filed by callback date. Computers often are used today with their automatic follow-up system.

Travel Agent Commission

The varying amount a travel agent receives from a supplier for selling transportation, accommodations, or other services. The average amount paid from hotels is 10% of the base rate.

Turn Down Service

Special evening service including removing bedspread and turning down the bed, straightening room and replenishing used supplies and linens. This is usually done in luxury type properties or for VIPs.

Twin

A room with two twin beds.

United States Travel & Tourism Agency

The former official U.S. agency for the promotion of travel to and within the United States and its possessions. USTTA was an agency of the U.S. Department of Commerce, but was closed down for funding and more likely political infighting in the 1990s. The national hospitality associations are lobbying to get a strong, viable entity established.

Upgrade

To move to a better accommodation or class of service at no additional cost.

Upsell

To offer a guest a better accommodation or class of service whereby the guest willingly pays a higher rate for the better level of service.

Valley Period

Also known as "off-season," valleys are times when demand for a property and its services is lowest. Reduced room rates are often offered during valley periods to attract business.

V.I.P. (Very important person)

A guest, who for a variety of reasons, has been designated by management to receive special treatment. Is usually pre-registered and should be escorted to room by a management representative.

Vacant and Ready

A room that is unoccupied, cleaned and ready for entering.

Wholesale Travel

An individual who specializes in putting tour packages together for individual Agent business and leisure travelers. These tours are usually marketed to the public through retail travel agents or the airlines.

"Walk" the Guest

A guest with a reservation, who cannot be accommodated is taken (gratis) to another property where a room has been procured and paid for by the "walking" property.

Walk-In

Person(s) requesting accommodations for that night who has no reservation.

Walk Out

When a guest leaves a property without paying his bill (Same as "Skips")

Yield management

See Revenue Management

◆ ◆ ◆ ◆ ◆

In an already open hotel where the expense meter is running anyway, and there are plenty of empty rooms in off-peak periods, somebody paying something is better than nobody paying nothing.

—*Claude Ballard, Vice President, Prudential Insurance*

(quote found in Educational Institute's Hospitality for Sale)

PROUD SPONSOR
of
HOWARD FEIERTAG
and
THE SALES CLINIC COLUMN
SINCE 1980

The archive of articles written by Howard Feiertag for *Hotel & Motel Management* is a treasure trove of hospitality sales and marketing jewels. Since 1980 Howard Feiertag has been dispensing his wit and wisdom in his monthly columns for our readers. Howard quickly became a reader favorite as his column has always been among the first read and most requested reprint in the magazine.

—Mike Malley
Publisher/Editorial Director
Hotel & Motel Management

(440) 891-3105
www.HotelMotel.com

Howard Feiertag is unquestionably the travel industry's foremost meetings expert and educator in terms of hespitality sales—whether within a big city hotel, a resort complex or aboard a cruise ship. His expertise and ability to communicate have made a tremendous difference in the travel world, and his professional approach has inspired others to follow his example.

—Joel Abels,
Editor & Publisher
Travel Trade

In choosing speakers, the Association tries to locate individuals who can present material in a solid, practical and entertaining manner. Rarely do we successfully achieve this, as was the case from your presentations. John, you exceeded the high standaards expected from speakers . . . . Once again, thanks for making our convention a huge success.

—Joss Penny
Director of Member Services
British Columbia Motels, Campgrounds, Resorts
Association

Lessons From the Field

In the storm of decreasing profit lines, higher employee turnover, increasing guest demands, more competitive hotels and shrinking availability of staff, John Hogan provides a calm shelter of management know-how for hoteliers. With great depth of hands-on experience in hospitality, John is able to help owners and managers devise solutions for the difficult challenges they face. In **LESSONS FROM THE FIELD** readers will find thousands of useful tips, all written with wisdom, humor and common sense.

—Aleta A. Nitschke, CHA
Publisher,
The Rooms Chronicle

ORDER FORM
For U.S.A.
See page 303 for Canadian Order Form

LESSONS FROM THE FIELD
PO Box 23177
Phoenix, AZ 85063-3177

I would like to order:

_____ copies of *LESSONS FROM THE FIELD*:

A Common Sense Approach to Effective Hotel Sales.

@ $29.95 U.S.	1-5 copies	_____
@ $26.50 (10% discount)	6-20 copies	_____
@ $22.50 (25% discount)	21 + copies	_____
	Sub-total	_____

Postage & Handling $3.00 for the first item ordered and $1 for each additional item. $25 maximum for volume up to 50 books.

Postage & Handling	_____
Total enclosed	_____

Check or money order only please, made out to:

LESSONS FROM THE FIELD.

Send to (please print):

Name _____

Organization_____

Mailing address _____

City_____

State/Province_____Postal Code_____

Lessons From the Field

ORDER FORM

For Canada
See page 301 for U.S.A. Order Form

LESSONS FROM THE FIELD
PO Box 23177
Phoenix, AZ 85063-3177

I would like to order:

_____ copies of *LESSONS FROM THE FIELD*:

A Common Sense Approach to Effective Hotel Sales.

@ $44.95 CAN	1-5 copies	_____
@ $38.50 (10% discount)	6-20 copies	_____
@ $33.75 (25% discount)	21 + copies	_____
	Sub-total	_____

Postage & Handling $4.00 for the first item ordered and $1 for each additional item. $25 maximum for volume up to 50 books.

	Postage & Handling	_____
	Total enclosed	_____

Check or money order only please, made out to:
LESSONS FROM THE FIELD.

Send to (please print):

Name _____

Organization_____

Mailing address _____

City_____

State/Province_____Postal Code_____

Lessons From the Field